It Happened In
Yosemite National Park

Remarkable Events That Shaped History

Ray Jones and Joe Lubow

Guilford, Connecticut

Project editor: David Legere
Map: Melissa Baker © Morris Book Publishing, LLC

Library of Congress Cataloging-in-Publication Data
Jones, Ray, 1948-
  It happened in Yosemite National Park : remarkable events that shaped history / Ray Jones with Joe Lubow.
    p. cm.
  Includes bibliographical references and index.
  ISBN 978-0-7627-5060-3
  1. Yosemite National Park (Calif.)—History—Anecdotes. 2. Yosemite National Park (Calif.)—Biography—Anecdotes. I. Lubow, Joseph M. II. Title.
  F868.Y6J63 2010
  979.4'47—dc22

                                                        2009039393

Printed in the United States of America

10 9 8 7 6 5 4 3 2 1

To Galen Clark and John Muir

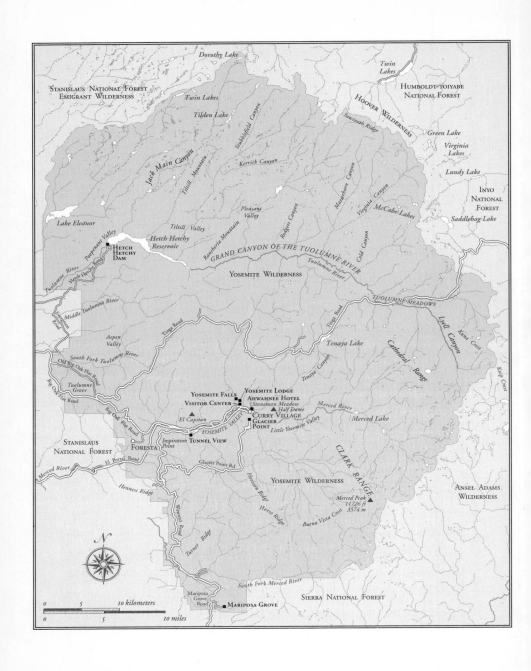

YOSEMITE NATIONAL PARK

CONTENTS

Introduction. vii

Paradise Sculpted by Ice—1,000,000 B.C. .1

Mariposa Battalion Invades the Valley—1851 5

End of Ahwahneechees—1853. 10

Galen Clark and the Giants of Yosemite—1857 15

Discovery That Helped Link Yosemite to the World—1870. 19

Great Yosemite Quake—1872. 24

Waterfall on Fire—1874 28

First Ascent of Half Dome—1875. 32

John Muir Rides a Wild Avalanche—1890 37

U.S. Army Saves Yosemite—1891 41

First Automobile in Yosemite—1900. 45

Death of a Legend—1902 50

Roosevelt and Muir Take a Hike—1903 .54

Vanishings—1909 to Present. 59

Tioga Pass Road Purchased—1915 65

Ansel Adams's First Photograph—1916. .69

Drowning a National Treasure—1923. 73

President Kennedy's Ghostly Rocking Chair—1962 79

Swept over the Falls—1970 83

War in the Valley of Peace —1970 87

CONTENTS

Crash of the *Lodestar Lightning*—1976 91

Tragedy Strikes Half Dome—1985 95

Paraplegic Conquers El Capitan—1989 99

Firestorm at Foresta—1990 103

Campers versus Bears—1996 107

Fatal Protest—1998 111

Young Climber Sacrifices Himself for a Friend—1999 116

Fatal Attempt to Fly Like a Bird—2001 120

Daring Blizzard Rescues—2004 124

Bibliography 128

Index 144

About the Authors 148

INTRODUCTION

When first-time visitors enter Yosemite National Park, they sometimes ask the rangers at the gateway booths to recommend an experience that will put the park in perspective. In response, rangers often recommend an overlook only a few miles from the park's western entrance. It offers a sweeping view of Yosemite Valley out toward El Capitan and beyond, and most find it so breathtaking that they cannot find words to describe what they are seeing. They invariably pull out their cameras, hoping that pictures may succeed where language is likely to fail. Probably it never occurs to them that by taking a picture they are preserving a view of Yosemite that is essentially unique. What they see today will look just a little different tomorrow. What they see tomorrow will have changed by the time the next day comes.

Nearly everyone who gazes out over the Yosemite Valley imagines that it is eternal. They believe that the valley has always looked much the way it does today and that if a reasonably determined effort is made to protect this national treasure, then it will never change. Certainly, there is much that has been and is yet to be done to preserve the beauty and natural integrity of this extraordinary place, but the notion that Yosemite is unchanging is completely mistaken. There is nothing static about Yosemite. It is a creation of nature and every bit as dynamic as nature herself. The only constant in Yosemite is change.

Yosemite did not begin as a canyon or even a river valley. It was born at the bottom of a primeval ocean a billion years ago or more. The land that is now Yosemite was lifted up when the floor of the Pacific began to push beneath North America, forming mighty mountain ranges, among them the California Sierra. And no sooner had the mountains begun to grow than rain, wind, and erosion began to tear them down again. As part of this process, the Merced and Tuolomne Rivers formed, cutting down into the Sierra granite. During the Ice Ages, these valleys were deepened and widened by the grinding action of ice sheets more than a mile thick. When the ice melted about 10,000 years ago, it left behind the spectacular canyons known to us today as the Yosemite Valley and Hetch Hetchy.

These transformations took place over a vast time span that may seem nearly infinite to a human being. It may take millions of years to create a canyon, but it takes only eighty years or so to live a human life. So compared to the processes of geology, our lives are hurried. People measure time in seconds, minutes, hours, days, years, or decades, and the changes we bring to a landscape take place over similarly short time periods. This explains why the pace of change in Yosemite increased drastically once people came onto the scene.

The first humans arrived in Yosemite a few thousand years ago. They were Native American peoples such as the Miwok, who lived mostly in harmony with their natural surroundings. However, neither the Miwok nor other Native American tribes who frequented the area left the land untouched. Often, they set fires to clear away forests and create open meadows to increase the population of game and improve hunting. They also planted crops and cut trees to build shelters or to burn in their campfires.

The pace of change increased yet again when people of European ancestry started filtering into the Sierra during the nineteenth century. The first such visitors to the Yosemite region are believed to have accompanied the famous trapper and mountain man Joseph Walker when he explored the area in 1833. Walker and members of his expedition are said to have stood atop a lofty cliff and peered down into a great Sierra chasm. This may or may not have been Yosemite Valley or the nearby canyon of Hetch Hetchy.

Walker and his companions could not find a way to climb down onto the floor of valley he described in his journals. Less than twenty years later, the armed troopers of the Mariposa Battalion had far less trouble finding their way into Yosemite Valley when they became its first official visitors. The battalion was not sent to explore Yosemite Valley, but rather to invade the homeland of the troublesome Ahwahneechee Miwoks and drive them out. Having completed their violent mission, however, they briefly surveyed the valley and were stunned by the grandeur of its scenery. The stories they told once they returned to the more settled parts of California generated an avalanche of interest in Yosemite, which soon came to be regarded as a land of stupendous natural wonders. And indeed it was. Yosemite had giant trees, mile-high cliffs, and waterfalls that plunged more than half a mile.

The big trees especially would fire the imagination of the public. Interest in these giant sequoias was so great that even as the Civil War raged in the East, Abraham Lincoln signed papers establishing a federal grant to protect them and the magnificent scenery that surrounded them. The grant, established in 1864, planted the seed from which one of America's most popular national parks would grow.

In the early days of the grant, when Yosemite was operated as a California state park, only a handful of visitors were able to make the arduous journey into Yosemite Valley and the nearby giant sequoia groves. Over time, a few rustic hotels were built and a few crude dirt roads opened to make access easier for horses, wagons, and tourists. Yet even after Yosemite was made a national park in 1890, visitors were still not flooding its roads and hostelries. Modern tourism was slow in coming to Yosemite, but by the twentieth century it had arrived. The first car—a version of the Stanley Steamer—chugged into Yosemite in 1900, the first airplane landed here in 1919, and the first truly modern hotel—the Ahwahnee—opened in 1927.

The park hosted its first visit by a U.S. President when Theodore Roosevelt spent four days here in 1903. Roosevelt did not stay in a swank hotel, but rather slept out under the stars with his guide, the noted conservationist John Muir. The experience made a powerful impression on the "Bull Moose" president and gave the cause of conservation a tremendous boost. Roosevelt would later sign legislation creating five more national parks and providing federal protection for millions of wild acres.

Roosevelt would not be the only president to see the park. John F. Kennedy visited the Ahwahnee in 1962 and brought the White House telephone switchboard with him! It is said by some that Kennedy's ghost still occasionally settles into a rocking chair at the hotel, producing nocturnal squeaks that cannot necessarily be explained as loose floorboards or creaky ceiling beams.

Yosemite is haunted by the memories of many other famous people—conservationists like Muir, scientists like Josiah Whitney, promoters like Oliver Lippincott, or nature photographers like Ansel Adams. It is probably safe to say that each has made an indelible impression on Yosemite while gaining something invaluable from it. However, the visitors who have brought the biggest changes to Yosemite are not presidents, intellectuals, artists, or celebrities of any stripe. They are average visitors who stream into Yosemite winter, summer, spring, and fall to behold the wonders that have captivated generations of Americans.

Approximately four million people visit the park each year. On an ordinary summer weekend the number of visitors in Yosemite Valley, once home to no more than a few dozen Native Americans, can reach 10,000 or more and rival the population of a small city.

With all those people on hand, a lot of things are likely to happen, some delightful, some terrible, some fascinating, and some tragic.

In a nature park with so many high elevations, so many narrow trails, and so much winter ice and snow, accidents are common. A considerable number of people have been swept over waterfalls or slipped on loose rock and fallen over cliffs. There have been fatal plane crashes and deadly traffic accidents. There have been a number of murders in Yosemite and quite a few suicides as well. And there have been an extraordinarily large number of disappearances. Sometimes in Yosemite hikers wave goodbye to their friends, head off down a trail, and simply vanish. Rangers search for them but never find a trace.

But most of the people who visit Yosemite don't get lost, at least not permanently. In fact, they may very well find something they've lost in the rush of their day-to-day lives back in more civilized places—themselves. Yosemite is a mirror capable of reminding us of our humanity and of our close ties to nature. It performs this miracle countless times each day in each and every tourist season.

As you'll discover as you read the following chapters, Yosemite is a priceless monument to glories of granite, water, and life, but it is by no means unchanging. A lot happens in Yosemite, some of it for better and some for worse. And in each story that is told concerning this grandest of all American national parks is a hint of the lessons and wisdom that can only be learned from nature.

PARADISE SCULPTED BY ICE

1,000,000 B.C.

Nobody knows exactly when it began, but about a million years ago the Yosemite area, along with vast stretches of North America, was hit by what scientists describe as a "snow blitz." The northern half of the continent grew colder, and so much snow fell during the winter that the sun could not melt it all before the end of summer. Over the years, the snow accumulated to great depths until it had buried the Yosemite region under a mountain of ice more than a mile thick. Inevitably, the ice sheet began to move, and mighty glaciers cut deep into the underlying rock. In time, the ice carved out the valley we see today, giving it the characteristic U-shape of a typical glacial valley.

Little else concerning Yosemite and its spectacular scenery could rightly be described as typical. There is no other place like it on earth. To make this clear to first-time visitors, Yosemite National Park rangers often send them to the Wawona Tunnel Overlook on Highway 41 only a few miles from the western park entrance. It's a great spot to take photographs, and plenty of people—droves of them, in fact—do just that. Others are too astounded by the view to use their cameras. They stand and stare with their mouths open as if they are about to recite a poem or deliver a philosophical speech on the marvels of nature, but most of the time, they say nothing. Indeed, is there any suitable thing that could be said? The view of Yosemite Valley from this place defies description. It cannot be put into words or, for that matter, captured on film unless, of course, your name happens to be Ansel Adams.

The Wawona Tunnel Overlook doubles as the trailhead for the steep hike up to Inspiration Point, but the less poetically named overlook provides inspiration enough for most. Mixed in with the inspiring view and the feeling of elation it engenders is a yearning desire to answer a single, simple but profound question. What great hand could have created all this beauty?

Scientists have a word for that hand. They call it geology. The slow geological processes that created Yosemite began long before the Ice Ages. In fact, the colorful rocks seen along the walls of the Yosemite Valley were deposited in sedimentary layers on a primordial seabed between 500 million and a billion years ago. The entire Sierra region, including Yosemite, was covered by an ocean at this time. Eventually, extreme pressures compressed the sediment into dense rock. Then, about 100 million years ago, the Pacific continental plate began to slip beneath North America, lifting the entire Sierra region and forming mountains. At the same time molten rock under the region began to solidify, creating huge blocks of granite. Today, one of those blocks stands guard at the western end of the Yosemite Valley and is so impressive it has been given a name. They call it El Capitan.

Originally, the land destined to become Yosemite National Park was made up of low, rolling hills and quiet streams, including the Merced River. The Merced is an old river, so old, in fact, that dinosaurs may once have relied on its slow-moving waters to ease their thirst. In time, however, the character of the once gentle Merced would change dramatically. As the Sierra Nevada range rose, the river grew into a destructive torrent, slashing at the rocks along its banks and carrying them in bits and pieces down toward the Pacific Ocean. Over millions of years, the Merced carved out a canyon as much as 3,000 feet deep. Then came the snow blitz and the Ice Age glaciers that cut even deeper into the rock, forming at last the valley we now know as Yosemite. When the ice finally receded about 10,000 years ago, the Merced River tributaries were left "hanging in the air," thus creating Yosemite's many spectacular waterfalls.

Of course, the snow blitz and glacial erosion theory is not the only explanation put forward for the creation of Yosemite and its many wonders. Yosemite's geological story has been told in a number of very different ways. Some have said Yosemite's mighty cliffs and canyons were left behind by a series of great floods, some of them of Biblical proportion. Others have argued that Yosemite's most prominent and rugged features were the product of repeated earthquakes.

During the mid-nineteenth century, the eminent geologist J. D. Whitney argued that the sheer cliffs and vertical walls of Yosemite Valley were the work of faulting. In Whitney's view, the earth had split apart, perhaps during a mighty earthquake. Whitney described this process in cataclysmic terms as a "wreck of matter and crush of worlds."

John Muir, who first visited Yosemite during the 1860s, saw its creation as a more gradual process. Muir was among the first to look upon the scarred walls of Yosemite Valley and conclude that they had been scoured by ice. Some say it was Muir who first proposed the glacial theory of Yosemite's formation.

There have been other theories as well. Recently, some geologists have proposed that glaciers played only a minor role in forming the

Yosemite Valley. They argue that rockslides and erosion can account for most, if not all, of the valley's most prominent features.

To this day scientists remain uncertain of the processes that created Yosemite. What we know for sure is that, during the Ice Ages, the valley looked very different than it does today. Then, when the ice finally released its grip on the Sierra Nevada, broad meadows began to fill the uplands and dense forests spread across the valley floor. With the grass and trees came the beaver, bear, and bighorn sheep, the deer, opossum, and chipmunk, the gray fox, woodpecker, and spotted owl. Eventually, people would come here, too, some with tomahawks, some with Bowie knives, some with cars, and some with cameras. No doubt, they've all brought along their questions as well. How could it be, they've asked? How could rock, ice, water, and time have sculpted this masterpiece, this paradise for speechless poets and philosophers?

MARIPOSA BATTALION
INVADES THE VALLEY

1851

Chief Tenaya of the Yosemite Miwoks, known as the Ahwah-neechees, looked out at his village with great concern for his people, who were struggling to find enough food to eat. As whites moved into the areas around Yosemite, first to search for gold and then to live and work the land, rivers, and hills for food, the Miwoks and other regional tribes had found their own food gathering limited to the point of starvation. Some of Tenaya's men had resorted to theft of livestock and had even raided trading posts in nearby white settlements. Whites had died in those raids, and Tenaya knew that all Native Americans in the area would be blamed. Yet he could not blame them for their deeds. They had been put to work in the mines by James Savage, the very same man who owned those trading posts. Savage had worked them long and hard and then refused to pay the wages he had promised them.

James Savage had decided in early 1850, after his trading post at the mouth of Merced River's South Fork had been raided by

"Yosemite Indians," that he would be wise to move his store to a spot along Mariposa Creek. He also opened an additional location on the Fresno River. Savage originally had come to California to serve in the war against Mexico in 1846. After the war, he settled in the Mariposa area outside of Yosemite Valley and established mines there during the gold rush. He learned the languages of the various tribes in the area and married a woman from each tribe as a means of establishing a bond between himself and the Indians and centralizing local power into his own hands. Having put many members of the Miwoks and Yokut tribes to work in his mines, he then branched out into trading.

The destruction of Savage's trading post was not an isolated incident. Although Savage had believed that his connections to the tribes would protect him, his native wives warned him that more attacks were coming. In an attempt to ward off these attacks, Savage took a local tribal chief with him on a business trip to San Francisco. Savage hoped that the chief would be overwhelmed by the number of people living in the city, and he would think twice about starting a war with a people who were so numerous and powerful. Once the chief saw the "big village," he would understand that there were just too many whites for a few scattered Sierra tribes to defeat.

However, Savage's plan never had a chance to work. While he was away, both of his trading posts were plundered, his goods stolen, and his buildings burned. What was worse, three local white men were killed during the attacks. Fearing for their lives and property, white miners and settlers in Mariposa County appealed to both the state and federal governments for assistance. These cries for help raised considerable alarm in Sacramento where, on January 24, 1851, Governor Peter Burnett authorized a military force, that would become known as the Mariposa Battalion. It consisted of 200 armed riders, each of them determined to put down the uprising.

Meanwhile a team of three federal "Indian commissioners" arrived, and in an attempt to defuse the situation, they began negotiations with the tribes. Most of the tribes participated in these talks, but not the mountain tribes of Yosemite, who mistakenly believed their fortress-like homeland was impregnable to invasion. Ignoring calls from both sides for peace, the governor ordered the battalion to advance on Yosemite and remove the Indians living there.

Having been given the rank of major and placed in command of the Mariposa Battalion, Savage sent an emissary to the Ahwahneechees demanding their surrender. They must leave the Yosemite Valley peacefully, he said, and come to a reservation established on the plains of Mariposa County where they would live among other tribes. Chief Tenaya refused and, pleading his people's case, made it clear that they would not long survive out on the plains far from their beloved Yosemite. His pleas fell on deaf ears, however, and Savage remained adamant. He threatened to destroy the Ahwahneechees if they did not comply with his demands. So, seeing no alternative, a deeply saddened Tenaya brought his people out of the Yosemite Valley and headed for the town of Mariposa, where, it was agreed, he would meet with the federal commissioners.

The evacuation got off to a rocky start as Savage noticed there were no young men amongst those who were leaving—only old men, women, and children. This strongly suggested that the tribe's young braves were forming a war party. Hoping to head off trouble, Savage took a small group of battalion troopers up the Merced River to search for the missing Ahwahneechees. This detachment entered the Yosemite Valley on March 27, 1851, and thus became the first whites to see the beauty and majesty of the Yosemite cliffs and waterfalls from the valley floor.

Dr. Lafayette Bunnell, a medical officer serving with the Mariposa Battalion, suggested they call this amazing place Yosemite, after the name given to Ahwahneechees by other tribes. Possibly the name was derived from a Miwok word meaning "grizzly bear." The name stuck as would the names Bunnell gave to many of the now familiar sights and features in the valley—Half Dome, for instance, or El Capitan.

While Savage's detachment dallied in the valley, Tenaya and his people had decided against their trek into Mariposa and escaped into the mountains. Unable to find the young Ahwahneechee men in the valley, Savage had now lost track of the entire tribe. The Savage expedition was rapidly deteriorating into a fiasco.

In an attempt to bring things under control, a second detachment led by Captain John Boling advanced into the valley. Boling's men soon captured five Ahwahneechees, including two of Tenaya's sons and a son-in-law. Boling sent one of the sons and the son-in-law to search for the chief and encourage him to surrender. They soon found Tenaya, and he agreed to meet with the whites. Before he arrived at Boling's camp, however, the three young Ahwahneechees who remained in custody there attempted to run away. One succeeded in escaping, but the other two were shot and killed, including the chief's youngest son. When Tenaya learned what had happened, the grief-stricken Ahwahneechee leader surrendered to his fate.

Boling's men set out immediately to find the remaining Ahwahneechees, eventually rounding up thirty-five exhausted and starving members of the tribe who were found huddled beside the lake that would later be named after Chief Tenaya. The prisoners were taken to a Fresno River camp for resettlement. Its job complete, the Mariposa Battalian disbanded on July 1, 1851.

Unable to adjust to life without the familiar foods and cool climate of his home, Chief Tenaya later appealed to authorities for the right to return with his family to the Yosemite Valley. Finally, he was allowed to go on the understanding that he would not break the peace.

Shortly thereafter, Tenaya's remaining followers in the Fresno River Camp slipped away and joined him in Yosemite. Unfortunately for the Ahwahneechees, the Yosemite they returned to, with all its beauty and rich resources, had been seen by whites and life there would never be the same. Their stay in Yosemite would be very short this time for they would soon be driven out again.

END OF AHWAHNEECHEES

1853

One summer's day in 1853, a young Ahwahneechee packed up the cremated remains of six fellow tribesmen and began a sorrowful journey. He then trekked from the lands of the Eastern Monos across the mountains to Hite's Cove, located well within the future boundaries of Yosemite National Park. Accompanying him was a small group of grieving family and friends comprising all that remained of the Ahwahneechees. They had much to mourn, for the remains they carried were those of loved ones, among them Tenaya, the last chief of the Ahwahneechee tribe. Tenaya had been their leader when they lived in Yosemite, and it was he who had tried so hard to help them resist the incessant pressure from white settlers and soldiers that had finally forced them to leave. Now he was dead. Once the procession reached Hite's Cove, the ashes of Tenaya and the others would be scattered upon the soil of the land the chief had loved. Then there would be a great "cry" lasting two full weeks—not just to mourn lost relatives or a lost chief but also a lost tribe.

The chain of events that led to this sad undertaking began when Chief Tenaya returned from a temporary exile with what was left of his tribe to Yosemite Valley in 1851. Having promised the local U.S. Indian commissioners that they would live peacefully, the Ahwahneechees tried to reestablish their lives in the supposed safety of the lush hills and valleys they knew so well. Unfortunately, the peace lasted less than a year.

In May 1852, eight prospectors entered the valley. Almost immediately, they were approached by a group of Ahwahneechees, who in a friendly manner, by all reports, told the intruders that they were trespassing and suggested that they should leave. After some discussion amongst themselves, the miners decided not to leave. Instead, they set up camp near Bridalveil Falls along the Merced River. Then, while several of the miners were away hunting and gathering wood, they were attacked by a group of armed men they believed to be Ahwahneechees. Two miners were killed in the attack, but three others escaped and managed to make it back to camp.

The reason for the outbreak of violence is unclear. Some say that one of the prospectors had purposefully incited the attack in hopes of ridding himself of some of his partners. Others say that Tenaya's men were retaliating for the death of a child, believed to have been caused by a prospector. Whatever had touched off the fighting, the surviving miners knew they were now in great danger and hurried away toward the west, carrying with them only their rifles and a bit of flour to sustain them during their journey.

The miners' escape proved an extremely narrow one. A second group of Ahwahneechees managed to intercept them in a narrow ravine, forcing them to scramble up a rocky slope while dodging arrows that whistled past and glanced off boulders. Taking whatever cover they could, the miners kept their attackers' heads down with well-aimed rifle shots. Then, after sunset, they slipped away in the dark and hurried off in the direction of Mariposa.

When they reached Mariposa five days later, the miners raised the alarm. There had been fighting with Indians in Yosemite! Hearing of the attack, other Sierra miners feared for their own safety and demanded immediate government action. Soon, a volunteer posse of twenty-five men returned to the scene of the fighting to investigate the incident and bury two dead prospectors. This they did without interference from the Ahwahneechees.

To prevent another war, the U.S. Army dispatched troops from Fort Miller in the San Joaquin Valley. Led by Lieutenant Treadwell Moore, the detachment entered the Yosemite Valley during the night and quickly captured five Ahwahneechees, all of whom were wearing some piece of white men's clothing. The Ahwahneechees did not deny they had taken part in the fighting but claimed they had done so in self-defense and in defense of their tribal lands. In no mood to bother with a trial, Moore ordered the summary execution of his five prisoners. They were shot still protesting that they had fought only to protect themselves and their families.

Hearing that soldiers had entered the valley and that five Ahwahneechees had been killed, Chief Tenaya fled with his people to the talus caves near what today are known as the Washington Columns. A few stragglers were caught and hanged by the soldiers, but most of the other Ahwahneechees escaped through the caves, which had outlets that led eastward. Although pursued by the cavalry, the remaining Ahwahneechees eventually reached the lands of a kindred tribe, the Piutes of Mono Lake. Hidden from the soldiers by the Piutes, the refugees managed to avoid further retribution.

The army expedition had an unexpected effect, one that would prove unfortunate for Native American peoples living in or near the mountains of the Yosemite region. Before returning to Mariposa

County, the soldiers spent time exploring the region around Bloody Canyon. An important mission of the Army of the nineteenth century was to survey federal lands, create maps, take temperature readings, note the types of wildlife, prepare samples of flora for study, and identify minerals. When the troops returned to Mariposa, they brought with them a wealth of information, including ore samples that led many to believe that vast new gold or silver deposits might exist east of the mountains. This in turn attracted many more prospectors to the area and placed increased pressure on Native American lands.

According to an account written by Dr. Lafayette Bunnell, who chronicled the Ahwahneechees' fight for survival, the tribe returned to the Yosemite area in 1853 and reestablished their settlements. The Monos had recently rustled horses from whites in the southern counties of eastern California and brought them back to their reservation to feed their population. Some of the younger Ahwahneechees then stole a few of the horses and took them to Yosemite. The Monos followed, and while Tenaya and his clan feasted on the horses, the Monos attacked, killing the chief by crushing his head. The women and children were taken as captives, while some of the men escaped. The older folk were left to fend for themselves.

The problem with this story is that Bunnell was writing from second- and third-hand stories he had heard concerning the incident. Years later, Ahwahneechees who had actually witnessed the events convincingly disputed Bunnell's account. One of those Ahwahneechees was Totuya, the granddaughter of Tenaya. According to Totuya, the tribe did not return to Yosemite while Chief Tenaya was alive. The chief had died at a feast after agreeing to compete with his Piute hosts in a "hand game," what we might think of as an intense form of wrestling. A test of physical and mental agility, strength, and focus, this game was commonly played by Native Americans, and in most cases led to no serious injuries. This time, however, an argument broke out, which led to real fighting, during which Chief Tenaya and five other Ahwahneechees were stoned to death.

These were the bodies that were cremated and carried to Hite's Cove. Following their two-week-long "cry," most of the remaining Yosemite Indians returned to live with the Monos. Others joined the remaining Miwok tribes along the Tuolumne River.

The Indian presence in the area that we know as Yosemite National Park lingered on, but life for these few residents had changed dramatically. They no longer followed their traditional Native American customs and had become dependant upon white management. Unable to move easily around Yosemite to gather food and other necessities as they had once done, many local natives became cooks, waiters, and laborers. They were paid in cash, which they used to buy food and clothing from white merchants.

By the 1930s, the native population of Yosemite had dwindled to a few dozen individuals. The National Park Service built a village to house these few families, but as the elders died, the children were not permitted to inherit the homes. The last resident Native Americans were gone from Yosemite by 1968. Today, their presence and those of their ancestors are remembered only in history books and in the stories told by guides to millions of Yosemite visitors.

GALEN CLARK AND
THE GIANTS OF YOSEMITE

1857

On a late spring day in May of 1857, a young hunter approached a backwoodsman named Galen Clark and told him a strange story. The hunter told Clark that in the nearby mountains he had come upon a spectacle so amazing that he would never have believed it had he not seen it with his own eyes. Clark was not sure that he believed it either, so he decided to go and see this intriguing sight for himself. What Clark found on the steep slopes above Yosemite's Wawona Valley would change his life forever. It would also change the way people everywhere related to the natural world.

John Muir once described Galen Clark as the "best mountaineer I ever met." Since Muir was considered by many to be the ultimate mountain man, these words of praise cannot be taken lightly. However, it could hardly be said that Clark was a born mountaineer. In fact, by the time he first came to the California Sierra, he was already well past the age at which most people's lives have taken a settled direction.

Born in Dublin, New Hampshire, in 1814, Clark received little schooling and did various types of manual labor before getting married and moving to Missouri during the 1840s. When he heard that gold had been discovered in the Far West, Clark had wanted to rush off to California, but the recent death of his wife made this impossible. It would take him almost five years to settle his family affairs, but in 1854, at the age of forty, he finally set out for the Sierra to try his luck in the gold fields. Like so many other prospectors, he found that luck was not with him. Instead of making a fortune, he contracted consumption, the lung disease we know today as tuberculosis. Edgar Allan Poe, the notorious gunslinger Doc Holliday, and countless others died of this malady during the nineteenth century. Clark's doctor told him he would die of it also. His affliction was so severe that he was given only about six months to live.

Not knowing what else to do, Clark set off into the high Sierra in search of what he desperately hoped would be a cure—pine-scented fresh mountain air. "I went to the mountains to take my chances of dying or growing better," said Clark, adding that he assumed his odds to be "about even."

His meager possessions loaded on the back of a burro, Clark retreated to the Wawona Valley. There he built himself a rustic cabin along the South Fork of the Merced River and attempted to recover what he could of his health. Occasionally, hunters and prospectors stopped by Clark's homestead to take advantage of his kindly hospitality. One of these wayfarers was the young man who sparked Clark's curiosity concerning what might lie in the hills just above his home.

Clark decided he would have to see this marvel for himself, and seized with an energy he had not felt in years, he set off into the mountains. With him was a friend, neighbor, and fellow homesteader named William Mann. When the two men reached the area the hunter had described, they climbed a modest slope, following for a time a small mountain stream. And suddenly, there it was—a tree unlike any Clark or Mann had ever seen. Mundane words like big or massive were useless for describing the tree, and indeed, Clark rarely used such adjectives when speaking of his first encounter with what we now call giant sequoias. Later, Clark would measure the tree and find that it was more than 15 feet in diameter.

The hunter had said there were three trees like this one. As it turned out, there were many such trees in what Clark and Mann agreed to call the Mariposa Grove, after the county in which it was found. In the presence of these great trees, Clark and Mann felt it appropriate to remove their hats and keep them off as if they stood in a mighty cathedral. "I was awed," said Clark, "and felt as never before the greatness of God's power."

Stunned by the magnitude of their discovery, Clark and his companion wandered from tree to tree. They saw what would later be called the Washington Tree (the largest in the grove, encompassing 36,000 cubic feet of wood), the Columbia Tree (at 270 feet, the tallest in the grove), the Grizzly Giant (at 2,400 years of age, the oldest in the grove), the Faithful Couple (two enormous companions with fused trunks), the Telescope Tree (a still living tree with a trunk completely hollowed out by fire), and many other such arboreal marvels. The first of the sequoias Clark and Mann came upon would eventually be known as the Galen Clark Tree.

Clark would never again be the man he had been before his walk through the Mariposa Grove. Despite the grim prediction that he would not long survive his consumption, Clark recovered his health and went on to live a long and fruitful life. In fact, he lived to the very ripe old age of ninety-six, an extraordinary life span in an era when most people lived only about half that long. Having been given the gift of so many unexpected years, Clark dedicated them to the

Sierra's scenic wonders. Partly as a result of Clark's discoveries, President Abraham Lincoln established a grant in 1864 setting aside the Yosemite and the Mariposa Grove for public recreation "to be left inalienable for all time." Clark was named "guardian of the grant," a post he would hold for twenty-seven years.

During the last years of his life, Clark removed a number of seedlings from the Mariposa Grove, transplanting them in a cemetery in Yosemite Valley not far from the foot of Yosemite Falls. He carefully nursed and watered the seedlings so that they grew into sturdy saplings. When he died in 1910, Clark was buried amongst these same young trees.

DISCOVERY THAT HELPED LINK
YOSEMITE TO THE WORLD

1870

One day during the summer of 1870, a group of construction workers made a discovery that would significantly alter the course of
Yosemite history. Hacking through dense forests to make way for a
wagon road in the hills west of Yosemite Valley, these hardworking
laborers came upon a sight that few of them could ever have imagined. There in front of them was a grove of immense trees. Some of
the trunks were so large that the workers could have built their road
right through the middle of them and left the trees standing. The
road builders might have cut down some of the big trees to clear a
path or they might have turned their road aside to go around the
trees. Instead, the amazed workers reported what they had seen to
their superiors. Their discovery was destined to play an important
role in the opening of Yosemite Valley to the outside world.

During the first years after the Mariposa Battalion invaded
Yosemite and then reported on the wonders they had found there,
only a handful of people attempted to visit the place and see these

sights for themselves. The main reason for this was that the Yosemite Valley and the high country beyond were almost impossible to reach. The only access was by way of nearly impassible river canyons and mountain passes, which none but the hardiest travelers could negotiate. Those sturdy few were well rewarded for the efforts, and having returned to civilization, they lavished praise on Yosemite's beauty and majesty. However, they also made it clear that their journeys to and from this earthly paradise had been extremely difficult. Such a trip should definitely not be attempted by the fainthearted.

Just reaching the foothills of the Sierra could be a daunting process. Starting in San Francisco, the typical tourist might travel by train, stage, wagon, or horse for as many as fourteen days to reach either Coulterville or Mariposa. There they would mount a horse or mule to begin an additional journey of two to three days over mountain wilderness to reach the valley floor. Because of the heights that needed to be scaled, many of these trails became impassable from late autumn until the spring thaw, and even during warm weather months, the trails and wooden bridges might be temporarily swept away by heavy rains and swollen rivers. Add to that the very real possibility of attacks by bears or other predators, both animal and human, and the obstacles standing in the way of a Yosemite visit became too much for most travelers to stomach.

Concerning just one of the many difficult passes that must be negotiated along the way, one early Yosemite tourist wrote:

> *The most difficult mountain in the way, after leaving Mariposa, is Chowchilla, some sixty-five hundred feet above the sea, and it is decidedly in the way, the trail over it being zig-zag in its course and exceedingly*

difficult. Up and up we went, struggling through dry dust and loose rocks surrounded by pine trees, Manzanita, and sage brush, the summit seemingly but a short distance, but when reached not there. We stopped and rested often in our ascent, and in about two hours we were on the summit, fatigued and jaded, as were our horses.

After 1864, control of the Yosemite country passed to the State of California and a board of commissioners appointed by the governor. The board agreed that Yosemite should be made more accessible to the public, but much of the responsibility for building roads was placed in the hands of private companies. Over the years several such companies were formed, each of them hoping to make fat profits by collecting tolls from travelers anxious to see and experience Yosemite's matchless scenery. Entrepreneurs began to compete with one another for the best routes.

Some companies had already built roads into the mountains. Most of these ended in mining camps and villages at the base of the foothills, but in the early 1870s, one of these enterprising young companies began a new road starting at Chinese Camp, intending to extend it as far as a key summit overlooking the Yosemite Valley. This was the Chinese Camp and Yosemite Turnpike Company, founded by George Coulter. The plan sounded promising, but Coulter ran out of money long before the road reached its destination. His company was then bought out by The Big Oak Flats and Yosemite Turnpike Company.

A rival firm called the Coulterville and Yosemite Turnpike Company had earlier built a road that ended at Crane Flat, joining Coulter's abandoned Big Oaks Flats road, and wanted to extend that road into the valley. The Coulterville Company was granted exclusive northern Yosemite Valley rights for a period of ten years during which time no competitor would be allowed to build north of the Merced River. Work began in 1870.

As the Coulterville company hacked its way into the wilderness, its workers came upon the big trees—giant sequoias—mentioned earlier and a decision was made to reroute the road in such a way that travelers could more easily reach the grove. This cost the company an extra $10,000 and delayed opening of the road to the summit above Yosemite Valley, which was finally reached on June 18, 1874.

Meanwhile, The Big Oak Flats and Yosemite Turnpike Company, hearing that the planned merge at Crane Flats with the new route wasn't going to happen, petitioned for another northern route into the valley. At first this petition was refused, but an appeal to the state legislature earned these upstart road builders a license. The race to the valley floor was on.

Both companies had to clear enormous hurdles in order to complete their roads. Rock had to be blasted and hauled away from the roadbed, which required heavy grading to make the road passable by wagon in either dry or wet weather. Each route had to negotiate grades of as much as 15 percent to lift them over the mountains. The route followed by the Big Oak Flats group's road required numerous switchbacks constructed by skilled Italian workers who had experience building roads in the Alps.

Ironically, the two companies finished their race to the floor of Yosemite Valley in a virtual tie. The two roads were completed less than a month apart during the spring of 1875, and each company could claim a significant victory. The Coulterville road offered toll-paying tourists a visit to the big trees, while the Big Oak Flats company provided its customers with the most direct route into Yosemite Valley.

Even as the roads were being built, tourist travel to Yosemite was on the rise. The length of time needed to make horse and mule trips into the valley steadily declined as each new segment of these roads was completed and opened to the public. By 1875, it had become possible to reach Yosemite and Big Trees Grove in a few days' time from San Francisco. Nowadays the same trip can be completed in an afternoon, but during the late nineteenth century, travelers must have regarded these dusty wagon roads as a marvel of convenience.

GREAT YOSEMITE QUAKE

1872

During the nineteenth century, people who lived in backwoods cabins in the Sierra went to bed early, just as most do nowadays. So the handful of hardy outdoorsmen and lonely innkeepers who occupied Yosemite and the surrounding wilderness were likely sound asleep and had been for several hours by the time the earth began to tremble at 2:35 in the morning on March 26, 1872. They would not remain in bed for long. In fact, most were dumped unceremoniously onto the floor, from which they quickly scrambled to their feet, if they were able, and ran for their lives.

It is hard to say what the earthquake sounded like down in Yosemite Valley. It may be that the high cliffs and the valley floor in between resounded like a mighty drum. Nearly everyone who heard the thunder of the quake and felt the earth roll from side to side was terrified and firmly convinced that the world was coming to an end. However, John Muir was not among these frightened individuals, or if he was afraid, his fears did not take charge of his senses. Instead, Muir was overwhelmed by curiosity.

"A noble earthquake!" he shouted and ran outside his modest Yosemite cabin to see if he could tell what was happening. "A noble earthquake!"

What had happened was this: Several dozen miles to the east and south of Yosemite Valley, the earth's crust had split wide open. Near the small town of Lone Pine in the Owens Valley, rocks were thrust more than 20 feet into the air, and the ground moved as much as 40 feet along the ancient Owens Valley Fault. This massive shift of rock and soil produced what is now estimated to have been one of the most powerful earthquakes in California history. If modern seismic equipment had been available at the time, it would probably have registered a temblor of 7.8 on the open-ended Richter scale. That's an earthquake roughly equal in power to the one that would devastate San Francisco in 1906.

Indeed, the destruction in Lone Pine and in nearby Owens Valley communities was nearly as complete as that visited upon the City by the Bay some twenty-four years later. But because the earthquake struck a lightly populated area, the damage was not as telling. Lone Pine was a town of about 250, not of several hundred thousand like San Francisco. It consisted of a hodgepodge assortment of fifty-nine crudely built houses and stores. By the time the earth stopped shaking, only a minute or so after it had begun, more than fifty of these buildings had been turned to rubble. More than one out of every ten Lone Pine residents had been crushed and killed by falling roofs and timbers. Similar ruin was visited upon towns and villages throughout the Owens Valley region.

In Yosemite, however, the earthquake had a less dire effect. This was true in part because Yosemite was farther from the epicenter of the big quake near Lone Pine, but also because there were fewer structures in Yosemite for the temblor to destroy. The earthquake nonetheless gave Yosemite a very severe shaking.

With the ground heaving this way and that, Muir found it very difficult to walk. For a time he braced himself against a tree. Then, as the shaking subsided, he moved into a clearing where he could get a better view of the valley's moonlit cliffs. Muir could hear rockslides and see columns of dust rising from parts of the valley floor that had been hit with large boulders shaken loose from the cliffs.

Among the Yosemite formations that fell victim to the quake was a well-known precipice known as Eagle Rock. Lodged high up along the south face of the Yosemite cliffs, it tumbled down in what Muir described as a "stupendous, roaring rock storm." The great friction generated by the impact of rock on rock threw up streaks of bright red sparks and started small fires here and there. Trees were torn up by their roots and smashed to splinters under thousands of tons of shattered talus.

Soon the air was filled with so much dust that visibility in the valley was reduced to a few dozen yards. This did not prevent Muir from continuing his inspection of the earthquake damage. Muir scrambled over enormous rocks still warm from the friction of their fall. He noticed that, mixed in with the dust, was the aroma of Douglas fir trunks that had been crushed and ground up by falling rocks.

Eventually, Muir reached the Hutchings Hotel owned and operated by Yosemite's legendary James Hutchings. Though damaged, the hotel had survived the quake. Even so, it was soon emptied of guests as everyone who could fled the valley on horses, mules, or whatever transportation was available. Many of those who raced out of the valley were only too well aware of the theory proposed by geologist Josiah Whitney that the Yosemite Valley had been created by an earthquake in the first place and that a subsequent quake might cause it to collapse into the earth all together. Understandably, no one wanted to be on hand if that happened.

Muir strongly disagreed with Whitney's theory, believing, as most geologists do today, that glaciers were responsible for the formation of the valley and its many spectacular features. Muir tried to calm the rattled nerves of hotel guests and permanent valley residents alike. In most cases he was unsuccessful, as nearly everyone who was able left the valley. Some had lost their homes and, discouraged by the calamity, decided to rebuild elsewhere in less vertical surroundings.

Among those whose residences were severely damaged by the quake was John Muir himself. Always more than comfortable sleeping in the outdoors, Muir made his home under the stars until he was able to build another cabin. Within a month he had completed a new home, placing it beside a clump of dogwoods near the Merced River. While aftershocks of the Lone Pine Earthquake continued for several weeks, they were of little concern to Muir. He neither expected another massive quake nor believed, as Whitney did, that the floor of the valley might collapse. Using his riverside cabin as a base, Muir continued his study of Yosemite's glaciers, compiling research to support his theory that mountains of ice, rather than earthquakes, had carved nature's great sculpture of Yosemite's.

WATERFALL ON FIRE

1874

One night during the spring of 1874, Yosemite visitors were treated to an extraordinary spectacle, a waterfall seemingly caught on fire! James McCauley, owner of the new Mountain House Hotel atop Glacier Point, had made a habit of building a large campfire each evening for his summertime guests. They would sit around the fire, laugh, sing, tell stories, and warm their hands and toes until almost bedtime. One night after everyone had gone back inside the hotel to escape the gathering mountain chill, McCauley decided to clean up the hotel grounds by kicking the remains of the campfire over the cliff. Apparently, many of the coals were still live since they flared up as they fell more than half a mile down to the bare rocks at the base of the cliff.

The long bright streaks of flame caught the eyes of many campers and nighttime strollers down in the valley. Everyone who witnessed this was delighted by the spectacle. To many it seemed as if the whole side of the cliff was lit up in a spray of flame. Some said it looked as if one of Yosemite's waterfalls had caught on fire.

When McCauley heard of this unexpected response, he decided to intentionally re-create what Yosemite visitors started to call the "Firefall" each and every night. He saw this as a way of attracting attention to his hotel and as a means of earning a little extra money. Each day McCauley's twin sons, John and Fred, were sent into the valley to solicit donations from park visitors, who gladly gave small sums to keep the spectacle alive. McCauley reciprocated by putting on the very best show he could manage.

Since, in those days, there was no set time for the event, McCauley would wave a flaming torch back and forth as a signal to spectators that the Firefall was about to begin. McCauley continued this tradition for more than fifteen years, but it was interrupted in 1897 when the innkeeper lost control of his hotel to a competing hotel owner from Wawona. For several years after that, Yosemite visitors who had seen it in the past were disappointed when they looked up toward Glacier Point in the evening and saw no campfire, no torch, and no Firefall.

In 1899 David Curry established a large public camping facility near the foot of the 3,200-foot Glacier Point cliffs. Curry heard glowing descriptions of McCauley's Firefalls from campground guests, and eventually he decided to stage the event himself. On holidays and other special occasions, he sent campground employees to the top of the cliffs to gather dry sticks, twigs, bark, and other kindling. At nightfall these combustibles were set on fire, allowed to burn down to glowing embers, and then dumped over the edge.

On those nights when a Firefall was scheduled, campground guests and other spectators waited with growing anticipation while the fire was built atop the cliffs. In this case the only signal that the Firefall was about to begin was David Curry's booming voice—so strong that it could be heard from the cliffs half a mile overhead—giving the command to let the show begin. The playful Curry readily admitted that he had a loud voice, so loud in fact, that he sometimes referred to himself as Captain Stentor, after the famous Greek herald whose commands, it is said, could be heard by an entire army. After warming up the crowd with a few well-chosen jokes and a story or two, Curry, in his guise as Captain Stentor, would look upward toward the cliff tops and shout "Let're go!"

The effect of Curry's Firefalls proved even more spectacular than those that McCauley's created during the 1880s and 1890s. The bright red and yellow streaks of flame often reached from the top of Glacier Point all the way down to the rocks at the base of the cliffs. Many attempted to take photographs of the Firefall, and images of it can be found in more than a few century-old vacation scrapbooks.

However, while campground guests and other park visitors took great delight in the Firefall and in Curry's antics, the United States Park Service was not amused. In 1913 park officials ordered Curry to stop putting on his Firefall show. Curry complied under protest and thereafter described Camp Curry as the place "where the Stentor calls and the fire used to fall."

By this time the Yosemite Firefalls had become world-famous, and visitors arriving at the park invariably asked about it. Rangers grew tired of disappointing them, and in a few years the Park Service reversed its no-Firefall policy. The shows were reintroduced during the 1917 summer season just as the U.S. troops began heading off to join their World War I allies in Europe, where they would see fireworks of a distinctly different sort.

Thereafter, the Firefall became an established Yosemite summertime tradition, and the show began each evening at 9:00 sharp. In Camp Curry, as the embers began to tumble down the face of the Glacier Point cliff, campers would sing the "Indian Love Call." At other campgrounds around the valley, they would usually sing "America the Beautiful."

The Firefall and many other traditional Yosemite Valley activities were discontinued during World War II. Some park service officials felt the Firefall was an inappropriate distraction in a natural area such as Yosemite and argued that the nightly performances should not be resumed after the war. However, they were overruled, largely because visitors wanted to see the show.

Postwar prosperity made it possible for more and more young families to own automobiles and take long vacations. Many picked popular national parks such as Yellowstone and Yosemite as destinations. Since the Firefall was especially exciting and attractive to children, it contributed to the family entertainment aspect of the park's offerings. However, more than a few visitors came to Yosemite Valley specifically to see the Firefall, and this added to the rapidly increasing problem of overcrowding. By the mid-1960s Yosemite rangers and park officials had had enough. In 1968 National Park Service Director George Herzog ordered the Firefalls stopped, and they have not been seen since.

FIRST ASCENT
OF HALF DOME

1875

It must have been very chilly up there on the mountain on that mid-October day in 1875, but the man standing on the summit was likely not cold at all. He had labored enormously over the previous two days to reach this eminence, a place where no human being had ever stood before. Now, flushed from his exertions and from the joy of having achieved his purpose, he held high an American flag, waving it furiously in hopes that someone in Yosemite Valley far below would see it. Perhaps he can be forgiven for his excitement, for he surely realized, as others would after, that he had accomplished something very special indeed.

Rising more than 4,737 feet above Yosemite's Merced River and some 8,842 above sea level is a mighty hunk of granite that looks as if it has been cut in half by some great upheaval. The impressive height and unusual shape of the rock make it a favorite subject among the countless thousands of photographers who flock to Yosemite National Park winter and summer. The rock in question is, of course, Half

Dome, and it ranks among the most widely recognized and celebrated geological formations in all of America.

Most park visitors believe that Half Dome was once a whole, rounded mountaintop and that some cataclysm, likely as not an earthquake, caused half of it to collapse into the valley. Geologists tell us that this is not actually so. In fact, Half Dome is about as whole as it has ever been, and the impression that a large portion of it has split off and fallen away is little more than an illusion. If Half Dome is viewed from the side, as from Glacier Point a few miles to the west, its true shape becomes obvious. Half Dome is not a dome at all, not even half of one, but rather a relatively thin blade of rock. Famed nineteenth-century scientist Josiah Whitney and other early students of Yosemite's turbulent geology recognized this.

Interestingly, it was Half Dome's craggy and nearly vertical cliffs that fall away on all sides from its summit that caused Whitney to declare that it could not be climbed. In 1869 Whitney wrote that "Half Dome is probably the only one of all the prominent points about the Yosemite that never has been, and never will be, trodden by human foot." He was wrong, of course, as is nearly always the case when people say that something can never be done. It would take a mere six years for someone to prove Whitney to have been mistaken.

The man who was destined to make the geologist eat his words arrived in the California Sierra without fanfare at some point in the early to mid-1860s. His name was George Anderson, and he was as undistinguished as Whitney was celebrated—Whitney's name would later be given to the highest peak in the continental United States. Unlike Whitney, who was a Yale graduate and a Harvard professor, Anderson had little formal education, but he would nonetheless make a profound contribution, if not to science, then certainly to the human spirit.

Little is known about Anderson's early life. It is believed he was born in the year 1839 in Montrose, a small coastal town in eastern Scotland. At an early age Anderson went to sea, perhaps because, like so many other young sailors, he wanted to see as much of the world as possible. Anderson would still have been in his early twenties when he alighted in California and set out for the Sierras to search for gold. Having about as much luck in the goldfields as most other prospectors, which is to say, none at all, Anderson eventually turned to other pursuits. It is hard to say how he made a living, but somehow he managed.

No one knows for sure what caused Anderson to attempt the impossible. He was living in or near Yosemite Valley during the 1870s, and it may be that when he looked up upon the cliffs each day and saw the mountain that could not be climbed, something inside him would say, "I can do that." Anderson began his assault on Half Dome little more than a week into October of 1876, America's centennial year.

Anderson was not the first to make the attempt. Half Dome is so prominent a part of the Yosemite skyline that it must have tempted more than a few climbers even in those very early days of Sierra tourism. In fact, a couple of years before Anderson's historic climb, master Yosemite trail builder John Conway and his two young sons fought their way to within a few hundred feet of the summit. The Conways pulled themselves partway up the long curve of Half Dome using a rope that they secured to bolts driven into the bare rock. This technique succeeded until they came up against a vertical wall of super-hard stone that would not yield to their bolts. Stymied by the mountain, Conway and his sons turned back. Likely they told themselves that Whitney had been correct, after all. Half Dome could not be climbed.

Having brought a stubborn streak with him from his native Scotland, Anderson refused to accept this verdict. Starting out sometime on or about October 10, he followed forest trails until he reached the old Conway rope, which had been left in place. Anderson used the rope to pull himself up to the point where the Conways had finally surrendered to the mountain. Likely he made several trips to carry up food, water, and other supplies, including plenty of additional bolts and rope. Then Anderson started climbing.

Instead of hammering the bolts into the rock, Anderson used a small hand drill to prepare a shaft. Then, having securely seated an eyebolt and tied his climbing rope to it, he would reach above his head and drill another hole. Once a bolt had been driven into the new hole, Anderson would tie a rope to it and pull himself up a few feet. Ascending the cliff in this slow and laborious manner, Anderson made steady progress. The climb is said to have taken at least two days, and by the time he reached the top, Anderson must have been near total exhaustion. Regardless of his physical state, the climber still found the strength to hold aloft the flag he had brought with him. Snapping in a high-elevation breeze, it waved for a while on what must have seemed to Anderson to be the top of the world.

The climber's extraordinary achievement would have a profound effect on his emotions. He would never again live far from Yosemite, and it seems his thoughts would never wander far from Half Dome. During the months and years that followed, he installed a permanent rope that enabled others to follow his path to the summit. He intended to put in a stairway as well but never managed to build it. What he built instead was a modest cabin that offered him a view of Half Dome. Occasionally, he would earn a little money doing odd jobs and acting as a guide for climbers. In 1884 he contracted pneumonia while painting a house in Yosemite Valley. Within a few days he was dead at the relatively early age of forty-five. A small granite rock marks his grave in the Yosemite cemetery. Perhaps a far more appropriate memorial is Half Dome itself, which is ascended regularly nowadays by climbers who use ropes, cables, and stairways installed during the early twentieth century by the Sierra Club. Anderson's rope was torn from the mountain by ice and snow a few years after he had placed it, but the memory of his magnificent accomplishment remains.

JOHN MUIR RIDES
A WILD AVALANCHE

1890

The start of winter in Yosemite can bring heavy snowfalls, and with them comes the danger of avalanches. The snowpack on slopes as steep as those above Yosemite Valley and in the Yosemite backcountry is highly unstable. It can break free and come thundering down without a moment's notice, sweeping up boulders and tree trunks and carrying away man-made structures and entire forests. When human beings get in the way of avalanches, the result is often death, either from slow suffocation under tons of snow or from being flung head over heels down the mountain and crushed. Nearly every year people are killed by avalanches in the Sierra, and more than a few have lost their lives this way in the Yosemite country.

John Muir understood better than most the dangers posed by avalanches. He had personally known people whose lives were ended by them. Like so many of the impressive natural phenomena he encountered in Yosemite, however, Muir respected avalanches, but he was not afraid of them. In fact, he gloried in them. They were, he believed, among winter's most fascinating spectacles.

One winter's morning in 1890, Muir set out into the Yosemite backcountry. He carried no pack and had no special equipment with him for he felt completely at ease in the wild and considered it his true home. Snow had fallen on the Sierra for several days running, and a thick blanket of it covered the inclines and ledges above the Yosemite high country meadows. There were sure to be avalanches, but unlike many winter hikers, Muir did not select a route designed to avoid them. Instead he was looking for avalanches so that he could study them and enjoy the show as they rumbled down the mountains.

Muir's objective that morning was a ridge soaring some 3,000 feet above the Yosemite Valley floor. From there he knew he would have an expansive view of the mountains and steep slopes all around Yosemite. He could hardly find a better vantage point for observing avalanches.

Starting at first light, Muir followed a familiar side canyon that he knew would lead him to the crest of the ridge. Whether taken in summer or winter, warm weather or cold, it was a beautiful hike, and Muir took pleasure in the lovely natural scenery that surrounded him. He had figured the climb would take three or four hours at the most, leaving him plenty of time to enjoy the view from the ridge and, if he was lucky, witness a few massive avalanches. However, the snow in the canyon was much deeper than he had thought, and the hike proved far more difficult than he had expected.

"Most of the way I sank waist deep," said Muir. "I sank almost out of sight in some places."

For hour after hour Muir struggled through the snow-clogged canyon and up toward the ridge. The sun rose toward zenith and then began to decline, and as the day wore on, Muir began to think he would not see many avalanches on this particular outing. With only an hour or so of sunlight remaining, he was still 300 feet or more below his objective.

"At this point my hopes were reduced to getting up in time to see the sunset," said Muir, but nature had a surprise in store for him.

As he reached the head of the canyon and started up toward the ridge in search of the best vantage point from which to watch the sunset, the packed snow gave way under Muir's feet. The outdoorsman tried to scramble out of the sliding mass of snow, but as he did this, even more of the weakened snowpack collapsed and headed down the mountain, carrying Muir with it.

Usually, when hikers or skiers are caught in an avalanche, it rolls over them, pulling them down as if they had stepped into quicksand. Survival may depend on their ability to roll their bodies into a ball and form an air pocket so that they'll still be able to breathe once the snow has buried them. Fortunately for Muir, however, the snow never pulled him under. Instead, he rode down the mountain on top of the snow as if body surfing an ocean wave.

"I was only moderately imbedded on the surface or at times a little below it," said Muir. "And as the whole mass about and beneath me joined in the flight, there was no friction, though I was tossed here and there and lurched from side to side."

Muir said he felt a sense of enchantment as he rode the plunging heap of snow. The experience may have reminded him of riding a wild horse, something he had often done as a hired hand on California ranches, but of course, what he was doing now—riding a wild avalanche—was even more exceptional. It was as if all the cares and restrictions that attend civilized life had fallen away in an instant and he had found himself firmly in the grip of natural forces that neither he nor anyone else could control. This would have terrified most people, but not Muir. All of his life he had seen nature as creative and benevolent rather than destructive, and no avalanche was likely to change his mind about that. Not this one, anyway. Why should it? Muir ended the experience without a scratch.

"When the avalanche came to rest, I found myself on top of the pile without a bruise or a scar," said Muir. "I had been swished down to the foot of the canyon as if by enchantment."

Muir lived until 1914, nearly twenty more years, and never forgot his wild ride down the mountain. It had been, he said, "an exhilarating and spiritual experience. Elijah's flight in a chariot of fire could hardly have been more gloriously exciting." Muir never tired of telling new friends and acquaintances about his ride and how it had taken him eight hours to climb to the top of the ridge, but only about a minute to get back down.

U.S. ARMY SAVES YOSEMITE

1891

When Abram Epperson "Jug" Wood, Captain in the United States Cavalry stationed in Arizona, opened his new orders, he was stunned. Wood was a veteran of the Civil War, a West Point graduate, and a career soldier with decades of military service. Much of it had been spent on horseback protecting wagon trains, fighting Indians, and guarding the Mexican border. Now his superiors were sending him and his "I" troop to San Francisco.

A man used to the wilds of the American West, to prairies, mountains, and deserts, Captain Wood did not relish his new urban assignment. Little did he know that San Francisco would serve only as a base camp. In fact, his finely honed skills in soldiering, diplomacy, and persuasion were about to be put to their greatest test in one of the orneriest places Wood might ever have imagined—the Yosemite.

The year was 1891, and the Yosemite had just been removed from control by the State of California and made a national park. It would be Wood's job to protect and maintain the new park in the name of the people of the United States and the federal government. This would not be an easy assignment.

Since the original federal land grant of Yosemite Valley to California in 1864, the condition of the valley and the surrounding mountains had deteriorated markedly. Yosemite was no longer a pristine wilderness. Roads had been built to bring in tourists, who expected amenities such as comfortable living quarters and good food. Hikers carried away souvenirs in the form of colorful rocks and flowers or limbs broken from trees—actual bits and pieces of the Yosemite. Trees were cut for firewood and pastureland was set aside for the horses and oxen that pulled the carriages and wagons that brought in the tourists and their necessities. However, the greatest damage had been done neither by tourists nor those who profited from them. Instead, it had been done by sheep. Flocks numbering in the tens of thousands had been brought into the region, destroying the natural balance, damaging delicate native plants, and denuding hillsides of the growth that protected the valley and other areas from floods.

Dismayed by the ongoing destruction of his beloved Yosemite, John Muir had called for a restoration of the valley and surrounding high country to its original, natural condition. With the help of his close friend Robert Underwood Johnson, the influential editor of the *Century Magazine,* Muir had pressed for establishment of a national park in Yosemite. By 1890, his effort had borne fruit, but it remained to be seen whether the Yosemite's new status as a national park would protect it from further damage or help restore the health of this wondrous natural area.

At that time, national parks were a new idea. The world's first national park was Yellowstone, established in 1872. It had been placed in the hands of the U.S. Army. Now the same would be done at Yosemite.

Running a national park may seem an odd job for the military, but it fits well with the mission assigned the military by our nation's founding fathers. From the beginning, the U.S. Army had been intended not just to protect the country from invaders or to keep the peace but also to explore wild lands and build up and protect the country's infrastructure. For instance, the famous Lewis and Clark Expedition in 1804–05 had been an Army operation. Both Muir and Johnson were happy to see the Yosemite placed in the care of the military.

Captain Wood understood that he faced a difficult situation. While he had authority within the national park boundaries, he had no powers at all on state-controlled portions of the valley. He had 760,000 acres of land to protect, yet only a handful of troops to patrol them. And the politics of the counties surrounding Yosemite—Merced, Tuolumne, Mariposa, and Madera—would pit the interests of the park against those of shepherds, ranchers, and businessmen determined to continue using the Yosemite for their own benefit. Many such individuals regarded the Army's arrival with deep suspicion.

On May 19, 1891, Wood's troopers established a seasonal camp along Wawona Road about a mile north of the town of Wawona. Another troop, under a different commander, was stationed near the great sequoia trees area. Wood started his negotiations with herders immediately, notifying them by letter of his intent to establish the park as a permanent wilderness, which meant that they could not use the lands for grazing. While that wasn't a problem for cattle ranchers, who kept their herds fenced in on their own lands, sheep herders needed to move their flocks from place to place to take advantage of fresh grass and fodder. Shepherds refused to acknowledge the right of the federal government to keep them and their herds off park land. With the support of local law enforcement officials, the shepherds brazenly ignored Wood and continued to bring their herds to the valley.

Wood decided to employ a strategy that had been very successful in Yellowstone National Park. His troops "arrested" the herders and took control of the herds. Then the herders were taken to one side of the park and released, while the herds were taken to the other end of the park and scattered. It took days and a great deal of effort for the herders to recover their sheep. Although it took years of such actions to stop misuse of the park by sheep herders, Wood's strategy eventually paid off, and the herds moved on to other grazing lands.

Wood's leadership proved key to establishing the Army's presence and the supremacy of the federal government over the lands within the borders of Yosemite National Park. He earned praise for suppressing forest fires, mapping and marking the boundaries of the park, and establishing new trails. Unfortunately he would not live long enough to enjoy his successes. Weakened by injuries acquired over decades of military service, his health failed, and he died in 1894. His replacement, Captain G. H. G. Gale, requested and was granted permission to change the camp name from Camp Wawona to Camp A. E. Wood.

The Army's presence became more-or-less permanent and lasted until the National Park Service was established and was capable of taking over management of the park on its own. During those years, the Army developed a management plan for the park, restocked depleted fishing streams, surveyed the park's natural resources, including flora and fauna as well as mineral wealth, designed and supervised construction of roads and bridges, and called for expanded acquisition of wilderness lands.

FIRST AUTOMOBILE IN YOSEMITE

1900

On June 24, 1900, something completely new came chugging and wheezing down a dirt road into Yosemite National Park. Neither the animals nor the people of Yosemite had ever seen anything like it. No doubt the first inclination of the park's wildlife—and likely many of its human inhabitants as well—was to flee into the forest. However, some curious Yosemite residents stood their ground. They wanted to see this newcomer, that is, so long as they didn't have to get too close.

The oddity that entered the park that day was nothing less than Yosemite's first automobile. As we now know, millions of others would come after, but this was the first. A steam-powered contraption mounted on a buggy frame, it rolled along on four skinny wheels with wire spokes.

Like most cars today, it was not a one-of-a-kind machine, but there were only a few like it. Part of a small line of steam-powered automobiles known as Locomobiles, it was manufactured in Connecticut under the direction of Francis and Freelan Stanley, creators of the famed Stanley Steamer. The Stanleys had been bought out by an investor who coined a new name for the Stanley firm. He called both the company and the cars it produced Locomobile, a name derived from the words locomotive and automobile. Only a few hundred Locomobiles were built during the company's early years of operation. Among these was the odd vehicle that rolled into Yosemite on that bright summer's day in 1900.

Driving the Locomobile into Yosemite was its mechanic, a man named Edward Russell. Riding beside Russell was his boss, photographer Oliver Lippincott, who operated the Art Photography Company in Los Angeles. There were no other passengers; there would have been no room for them anyway since the little Locomobile barely had seat space for two men sitting side by side.

Lippincott owned the Locomobile and had a business relationship with the company that built it. He had agreed to promote the advantages of the Locomobile and, by extension, of other personally owned and driven vehicles—what today we might call family cars. At that time the idea that average families might own something as newfangled as a motor-powered vehicle was still strange to most Americans. After all, why purchase a car if you already owned a good horse or mule? Lippincott's Yosemite visit was intended to provide at least one answer to that question.

Lippincott intended to prove that Locomobiles and other automobiles would make it possible for ordinary people to visit distant holiday destinations such as national parks. To convey this concept to the public, he would not only travel in his Locomobile to Yosemite but also take pictures of the car parked beside or on top of many of the park's most famous features. Automobile manufacturers still make effective use of this technique today by running magazine and television advertisements that frame their shiny new models in a spectacular natural setting. Lippincott's approach to the market

would take a simpler path. His company in Los Angeles would pub-
lish the pictures, sell them at a profit, and in this way, promote both
the Locomobile and Yosemite.

Lippincott and his mechanic entered Yosemite by way of
Wawona, rattling along the rough dirt roads that led to the Mariposa
Grove and Yosemite Valley. At the various hotels they visited, they
were greeted by crowds of animated tourists and Yosemite residents
who pummeled them with questions about their vehicle: "How fast
does it go? How do you steer it? How do you stop it? How do you
feed it? How do you keep it from running amok?" Lippincott and
Russell answered as best they could, laughing and joking with the
curious and taking anyone who dared for short rides in the car.

The Locomobile would remain in Yosemite National Park for
several weeks while Lippincott photographed the spindly little car in
the Big Trees, at El Capitan, and at many other park locations. In
some ways, these outings resembled modern advertising photo shoots
except that there was little equipment and very few props or extras.
Even so, Lippincott was serious about the work. It is said he might
take several hours setting up a shot.

For one of Lippincott's Yosemite photography sessions, Russell
drove the Locomobile up the steep and winding Glacier Point Road
to the Mountain House Hotel, a process that took more than five
hours. He and the photographer arrived after dark and checked into
the hotel. After sunrise, the Locomobile was driven out to Glacier
Point's famed Overhanging Rock. Rather than risk driving the
vehicle out onto the rock under its own power, it was pushed into
place by several strong men. Each of them had a rope tied around his
waist for protection in case of a fall.

"The women watching this buried their heads in their hands,
horrified at the sight," Lippincott later said. "I firmly believe that
if the machine had gone over, every man of the party would have

gone with it. They all hung on while the camera was adjusted, and I believe no picture was ever so long in being taken."

Lippincott's photography expedition to Yosemite proved successful. The pictures he took were very popular at the time and likely made lots of money for everyone concerned. Nowadays, an original of one of these Lippincott photographs may sell for many thousands of dollars.

While he may have been the first, Oliver Lippincott would certainly not be the last photographer to use Yosemite's spectacular scenery to highlight a modern motor vehicle. In one fascinating instance, Arthur Pillsbury drove his brand-new Studebaker to Glacier Point for a photo shoot in September 1916. His aim was to take his own version of Lippincott's Locomobile picture on Overhanging Rock. Having driven to Glacier Point, he tried to take the Studebaker out onto the overhang, but several large boulders blocked his path. To overcome this obstacle, Pillsbury hired several carpenters then working on the Glacier Point Hotel. The carpenters built a small but sturdy trestle, and once it was complete, the Studebaker was rolled into position and duly photographed. One of the pictures taken that day features Pillsbury himself straddling the hood.

As anyone who has visited Yosemite during the last half century or more knows only too well, automobiles are no longer a rarity in the park. More than four million people visit the park each year, and while many arrive in buses or use other types of transportation, most drive into the park in their own automobiles. On summer weekends, roads into Yosemite Valley can resemble a Los Angeles freeway at rush hour. Traffic inside the valley often moves at a snail's pace, and parking can be scarce. Various plans to limit the number of cars inside the valley at any one time have been implemented. These include a special fee for bringing a car inside the park and the offer of shuttles to make entering the park and moving around inside the valley an automobile-free experience. Still, it seems extremely unlikely that cars will ever be completely banned from Yosemite. For better or worse, Americans tend to identify their national parks with the personal freedom and mobility offered them by their cars. They began to make this link on the day that Lippincott and Russell brought their hissing steamer into Yosemite.

DEATH OF A LEGEND

1902

On a lovely late autumn day in the California Sierra, James Mason Hutchings and his wife, Emily Edmunds, were enjoying an experience that generations of tourists have cherished. Headed into Yosemite National Park, where they hoped to enjoy a weekend camping trip, they had just caught sight of the majestic, natural stone tower known as El Capitan. Descending toward the big rock in their horse-drawn buggy, they gloried in the expansive views of Yosemite Valley. As Edmunds would later describe the experience, the scenery impressed them "beyond all expression." Unfortunately, this spiritually uplifting journey was destined to end in tragedy. It was 5:00 in the afternoon on October 31, 1902, and the two travelers were about to be involved in one of the most unusual—and historic—roadway accidents in Yosemite's long and eventful past.

In one way or another, Hutchings had been caught up in dramatic events nearly all of his life. Born in England in 1820, Hutchings arrived in California in 1849 at the height of the gold rush. A capable man who was sure of his instincts, Hutchings headed for the

Sierra foothills to try his luck as a prospector. Unlike so many other hopeful forty-niners who went bust without ever finding any gold, Hutchings struck pay dirt and returned to San Francisco a rich man. The fortune he had made in the mountain gold fields and mines would not remain intact for long, however. Hutchings soon lost every nickel of it in a calamitous bank failure.

To recoup his fortune, Hutchings turned to publishing and proved no less capable with pen, ink, and paper than he had been with a pick, pan, and shovel. Writing and publishing articles extolling the wonders of California, Hutchings captivated thousands with his flowery descriptions of western scenery, and by the mid-1850s he was once more a wealthy man. Hutchings's favorite subject was California's Sierra Nevada, and he devoted the *California Magazine* he had founded almost entirely to popularizing the spectacular scenery of these rugged mountains.

In 1855 Hutchings led a small group of curious travelers on an expedition to Yosemite. They would be among the very first tourists ever to set eyes on Yosemite Valley. Hutchings later described the experience this way:

> *Descending towards the Yo-Semity Valley, we came upon*
> *a high point, clear of trees, from whence we had our first*
> *view of this singular and romantic valley. As the scene*
> *opened in full view before us, we were almost speech-*
> *less with wondering admiration at its wild and sublime*
> *grandeur.*

One of the travelers accompanying Hutchings that day was so stunned at the sight that he asked if they had come to "the end of all things." Perhaps it seemed to him that he and his fellow travelers were approaching the gateway to infinity. How could anything less be so beautiful? For Hutchings, however, this moment certainly was not an ending. Rather it was yet another new beginning for a man who would experience many of them in his life.

From this moment forward and for decades thereafter, Yosemite would be the focus of all Hutchings's activities. He led other groups of tourists into the Yosemite country and focused his magazine upon its many wonders. In 1864 he bought the Upper Hotel, which had been built a few years earlier to accommodate the steady flow of adventurous tourists that his publication helped encourage. Coincidentally, just ten weeks later President Abraham Lincoln would sign the bill that made Yosemite one of America's largest public recreation areas. Some say this might never have happened without the publicity that Hutchings had given the valley through his writings.

Although he eventually sold his hotel, Hutchings lived in the Yosemite Valley for the better part of fifteen years. While there he wrote several books, including *Scenes of Wonder and Curiosity in California* and *In the Heart of the Sierras,* which is filled with information on Yosemite and descriptions of its scenery. As a result, Hutchings's name became so closely linked to the park and to efforts to preserve the surrounding wilderness that he was named "Guardian of Yosemite" by California state officials.

Although it pained him to do so, Hutchings eventually left Yosemite to take over as innkeeper of the Calaveras Big Tree Grove Hotel east of Sacramento. There he married Edmunds, his third wife. Hutchings was extremely anxious to show her Yosemite, and in 1902, at the age of eighty-two, he got his chance. A brief vacation from their duties at the hotel provided Hutchings and the much younger Edmunds an opportunity to travel, and not surprisingly, they ended up heading down the road to Yosemite.

The descent into Yosemite Valley proved more difficult than Hutchings remembered, but his hands were still strong and he kept a tight rein on the buggy's two horses as he negotiated the hairpin turns and steep inclines. He and Edmunds had almost reached the valley floor—and safety—when something completely unexpected happened. Apparently, a coyote, fox, or some other creature dashed out of the woods and spooked one of the horses. The frightened horse reared and then galloped off down the hill toward the base of El Capitan. The other horse joined in, and though Hutchings pulled back on the reins with all his strength, the buggy and its passengers were whisked along in a wild ride toward almost certain disaster.

The buggy careened around one turn and then another while swaying from side to side. Hutchings shouted a warning to his wife, telling her the buggy was out of control and that she should brace herself for a crash. With the sheer wall of El Capitan looming before them, the horses seemed to slow a bit, but it was too late. One of the buggy wheels struck a large rock and sent Edmunds flying into the weeds. Hutchings held the reins for a moment or two longer, but then another severe jolt pitched him forward over the front of the buggy and into a cluster of granite boulders. Almost miraculously, Edmunds was uninjured, but when she reached her husband's side, she founded him battered, bleeding, and barely conscious.

"I fear I am very much hurt," said Hutchings, an assessment that proved all too accurate. In fact, those were his very last words. Edmunds gave him a shot of whiskey in hopes of reviving him, but Hutchings lapsed into a coma and within minutes the legendary Yosemite promoter and protector was dead. Two days later Hutchings was laid to rest beneath a stone cross in the Pioneer Cemetery of his beloved Yosemite. He would, of course, never leave the valley again.

ROOSEVELT AND MUIR TAKE A HIKE

On the evening of May 15, 1903, two middle-aged men set up camp beside the massive trunks of the sequoias in Yosemite's Mariposa Grove. One of them built a fire while the other gathered ferns and fallen plumes of greenery from the big trees to soften their beds. Then the campers settled down for the night and, no doubt, drifted off to sleep gazing up at tree limbs that seemed to reach halfway, at least, to a sky pocked with glittering stars.

Countless Yosemite outings have begun in this same enchanted manner or in one very similar, but this camping trip was unlike any that had come before or would come after. What set this wilderness evening apart was the identity of the campers. One was John Muir, who by this time was a widely published and renowned naturalist, a man who many considered the founder of the American conservationist movement. The other, also a conservationist, was none other than President Theodore Roosevelt.

When, as vice president, Roosevelt ascended to the presidency after the assassination of William McKinley in 1901, he brought with him a deep and abiding interest in the outdoors and in conservation. Roosevelt believed that the human spirit must be nourished, not just by religion or philosophy but also by exposure to nature. Therefore, it was in the national interest and in the interest of each and every citizen to preserve as much as possible of America's grand scenic wilderness. This point of view drew Roosevelt to thinkers and writers such as John Muir, and the president read Muir's books and articles with great interest.

In 1903 Roosevelt announced that he planned to visit California to inspect the federal lands there and enjoy the region's famed natural wonders. High on his agenda was a stop in Yosemite. Roosevelt wrote a personal letter to Muir asking if the reclusive, but increasingly well-known naturalist would serve as his guide.

"I do not want anyone but you," said Roosevelt. "I want to drop politics absolutely for four days and just be out there in the open."

Extraordinary as it may have seemed, it sounded very much as if the President of the United States had in mind a camping trip, and what better place for such an outing than Yosemite? Muir was deeply honored by the president's request and quick to see in it an opportunity to put forward his own conservationist ideas, particularly those related to preservation of the California Sierra. Muir eagerly accepted the president's proposal, and the expedition was set for mid-May in 1903.

On May 15, President Roosevelt arrived in the tiny town of Raymond just south of Yosemite and, accompanied by Muir, rode by stagecoach to the Mariposa Grove. After a walk through the awe-inspiring big trees, Roosevelt sent for his luggage which had been transferred to a comfortable if not elegant hotel in Wawona. California officials were certain Roosevelt would want to spend the night in a good room with heat and running water. In fact, members of the Yosemite Commission had hoped to wine and dine the president while promoting their own commercially oriented plans for Yosemite. They would be bitterly disappointed. Roosevelt slept on the ground that evening just as he would for the next several nights.

Roosevelt later described the adventure this way:

> *John Muir met me with a couple of packers and two mules to carry our tent, bedding, and food for a three days' trip. The first night was clear, and we lay down in the darkening aisles of the great Sequoia grove. The majestic trunks, beautiful in color and in symmetry, rose round us like the pillars of a mightier cathedral than ever was conceived even by the fervor of the Middle Ages. Hermit thrushes sang beautifully in the evening, and again, with a burst of wonderful music, at dawn.*

On the following day, Roosevelt and Muir rode on horseback to Glacier Point. As they approached the summit, the horse's hooves broke through thin crusts of snow and ice. Roosevelt spent so much time enjoying the spectacular view from the south rim of the valley that he and Muir decided not to continue down the trail. Instead they pitched camp in a clump of trees near the cliffs. Muir built a fire, which he used to brew a steaming pot of coffee and barbecue a pair of plump beefsteaks that had been packed in for the occasion. Smelling the coffee and hearing the sizzle of the steaks, the president expressed characteristic Roosevelt enthusiasm. "Now this is bully," he said.

When Muir and Roosevelt woke the next morning, they found their bedding and the ground all around their campsite covered in a blanket of snow. After breakfast, they pushed on down into the valley. There an official party waited, anxious to welcome the president with a reception, banquet, and evening fireworks, but it was not to be. Ignoring local politicians who hoped to spend the evening currying favor with him, Roosevelt set up camp near El Capitan. He had said he wanted to leave politics behind on this trip, but he had some serious questions to ask John Muir. The Yosemite Valley was not the pristine natural paradise he had hoped to find. It had obviously suffered from lumbering, agriculture, grazing, and abuse by tourists and commercial interests. What could be done to help?

Muir had a ready answer for the president's question. He believed Yosemite could not be adequately protected while under state control. A generation earlier, Congress had granted the State of California the authority over activities on public lands in Yosemite. This left Yosemite Valley in particular at the mercy of local politics and local interests. Muir believed the only way to save Yosemite was to place all of it under federal control.

However, when the camping trip ended the next day, Muir was still not sure he had convinced the president of the need to place Yosemite Valley—"the grandest of all nature's temples"—in federal hands. By the time Muir and Roosevelt parted, the president had made no firm commitments. "Goodbye, John," said Roosevelt. "Come and see me in Washington. I've had the time of my life."

Later, Muir had nothing but good things to say about Roosevelt. "I had a perfectly glorious time with the president and the mountains," he told his friends. "I never had a more interesting, hearty companion."

But Muir would have to wait and see if his campfire chats with the man many even then regarded as one of the greatest American presidents would prove of any practical benefit for conservation in general and Yosemite in particular. As it turned out, the wait and the camping trip proved well worthwhile. Roosevelt, whom many called T. R. but only close friends and associates dared call Teddy, would serve six more years as president. By the time he left office in 1909, he had added 148 million acres to the national forest system, created sixteen national monuments, and established five national parks. Perhaps most importantly from Muir's point of view, Roosevelt made Yosemite Valley part of Yosemite National Park. Upon hearing this, Muir responded with these words: "Bully for Teddy Roosevelt!"

VANISHINGS

1909 to Present

A young man camping in Yosemite with friends pulls on his hiking boots, lifts a pack onto his back, and sets off down an inviting trail. He tells everybody that he won't be away for long. He's just going out for a short walk to stretch his legs and take in a little of the park's abundant fresh air and natural beauty. After a few hours, his friends begin to wonder what's taking him so long. Didn't they all have dinner plans? After a couple more hours, they begin to worry. Later that night they flag down a park ranger cruising by in his patrol car. He tells them that the young hiker has probably gotten lost or decided to spend the night out on the trail and that he will likely show up in the morning.

By the time the sun clears the eastern peaks, the missing hiker has still not returned to camp. His friends are really alarmed now, and they contact park authorities. Soon, rangers are riding up and down roads and searching Yosemite's far-flung trail system searching for the missing hiker. The search goes on for days, but after a week or so, it winds down, and no trace of the young man is ever found.

This is an old and tragic Yosemite story, and it has been repeated over and over for generations. Dozens, perhaps even hundreds, of people have disappeared in the vastness of the Yosemite backcountry. Sometimes their remains are located, and investigators conclude that they slipped on a rock and took a fatal fall, froze to death in the snow, or drowned in a deep pool. In many cases, however, these missing people have vanished completely, leaving behind no clothing, camping gear, or remains as clues to their fate.

One of the first such incidents noted in park history took place on June 17, 1909. Late on that afternoon, a San Francisco jeweler named F. P. Shepherd left the Glacier Point Hotel and walked off toward Sentinel Dome about a mile away. At first Shepherd was accompanied by a pair of young female companions, but they soon tired of the hike and returned to the comfort and warmth of the hotel to await him. Their wait would turn out to be a very long one indeed. Before Shepherd's friends headed back to the hotel, they had bid him farewell and watched him walk off into the thick fog that had set in over the Yosemite cliffs. Shepherd disappeared into that fog, and although they didn't know it at the time, he would never be seen again.

When he failed to return to the hotel that evening, his friends alerted their innkeepers who, in turn, notified park authorities. Nothing more could be done before morning, but on the next day, U.S. Cavalry riders began a search of trails, meadows, and canyons surrounding Sentinel Dome. They were extremely thorough, using rope ladders and grappling irons to scale cliffs and scramble down into hidden ravines. They risked their own lives to find Shepherd and, perhaps, save him, but it was all in vain. He had vanished without a trace. A few days later the cavalry officer in charge of the search called it off, concluding that Shepherd was now "beyond human aid." In his official report on the incident, he suggested that Shepherd may have gotten lost in the fog, panicked, and run helter-skelter through the brush before pitching headlong over one of Yosemite's towering cliffs. In truth, no one knew for sure what had become of Shepherd, and his body was never found.

Many, if not most, of the other disappearances in Yosemite are equally mysterious. Most involve solo hikers, people who decide to take their chances in the wilds of Yosemite without a companion. Park rangers often warn hikers not to go on long walks along trails or in the backcountry without a friend. The reasons for this should be obvious. If a lone hiker becomes ill or is injured in a fall or some similar accident, there will be no one to assist or go for help.

Even so, Yosemite's great natural beauty can be a powerful inducement for a hiker who may not have a friend to come along on a walk. One such hiker was Frank Koenman, an amateur photographer from San Francisco who rented a tent in Camp Curry on the night of May 31, 1925. Over the next ten days, he was often seen around the camp or along trails carrying his camera equipment, apparently in search of the perfect nature photograph. Koenman was always alone on these occasions.

On or about June 11, Koenman's acquaintances at Camp Curry noticed that he was gone, but no one thought anything of it. In Yosemite people come and go all the time, and anyone who had met Koenman in the park assumed he had returned to his job and life in the big city. Then, on June 18, Koenman's employers called Camp Curry to ask about him. He had been due back at work several days earlier but had never shown up.

Campground employees checked Koenman's tent and found there a suitcase, a camera case, and an assortment of photographic supplies but no sign of the camper himself. Park rangers initiated a search but had only the vaguest idea of where to look. Some campers said they had seen Koenman on or about June 11. Apparently he had told them he was headed for Inspiration Point to take some photographs. Others said they he had seen him strap his camera to his back and head off in the direction of Yosemite Falls. The trails leading to Inspiration Point and Yosemite Falls were thoroughly searched, but no trace of Koenman was ever found.

Many other Yosemite visitors have gone missing under similar circumstances. For instance, Godfrey Wondrosek vanished while on a solo hike to Half Dome in April of 1933. A twenty-six-year-old tourist from Chicago, Wondrosek was reported missing by his sister, who was vacationing with him in the park. Nearly a week of searching trails in the area of Half Dome revealed nothing.

In 1954 Walter Gordon, a University of California researcher and experienced hiker, set out from Camp Curry carrying a boxed lunch, which he intended to eat somewhere along Yosemite's Ledge Trail. He never returned. The search effort included one of the first uses of a helicopter inside the park, but no sign of Gordon was found.

In 1976 a young Yosemite bus dispatcher named Jeff Estes hiked solo to Lake May, where he meant to spend the night. He told friends he intended to hike back down along the Snow Creek Trail and return to his lodgings the following morning. He never arrived. An extensive four-day search revealed nothing.

Lone hiker Tim Barnes set off along Murphy Creek Trail on the morning of July 5, 1988, and never returned. An outdoor enthusiast from Cucamonga, California, the twenty-four-year-old Barnes had told friends he intended to walk to Polly Dome Lakes a few miles up the trail. He said he would return by late afternoon, but by nightfall no one had seen him. A wide-ranging air and ground search failed to locate either the living hiker or his remains. According to an official accounting of the unsuccessful search, it would end up costing the park more than $175,000.

A few months after young Barnes vanished, a much older hiker named Donald Buchanan disappeared while hiking near Half Dome. Buchanan was eighty-six years old and in very poor health. In fact, he was dying of cancer, a circumstance that eventually led authorities to believe that he had committed suicide. Searchers found the remains of a campfire that he was believed to have built. They also found his wallet and his false teeth but were unable to locate his body. Poignantly, Buchanan had loved the Yosemite backcountry and spent more than half his life hiking it. Perhaps he simply wished to spend his last moments in his favorite place.

Walter Reinhart, another hiker with lots of experience on backcountry trails, was thought to have set off alone along a trail above White Wolf on or about September 20, 2002. Wherever Reinhart may have chosen to walk that day, he never returned to claim his vehicle, which was found at the White Wolf trailhead. Reinhart was sixty-six, but his friends said he was in excellent physical condition. A former U.S. Marine, he had been trained to survive in the wilderness, but something must have happened to him that taxed his survival skills to the breaking point. A weeklong search by park rangers turned up no trace of him. A second search carried out by Marines with training in mountain warfare also failed to produce any clue to Reinhart's whereabouts or his ultimate fate.

In mid-June of 2005, fifty-one-year-old Michael Ficery of Santa Barbara pulled on a heavy pack and hiked alone into the backcountry north of Hetch Hetchy. He would never be seen again. Although it was the beginning of summer, there was still plenty of snow in the high country, so much of it in fact, that many trails were extremely hard to follow. When Ficery went missing, rangers assumed he had gotten lost in the snow, but their massive search-and-rescue effort produced no results. Helicopters were used to drop off search parties at strategic points in the mountains. In all, more than $450,000 was spent in an unsuccessful attempt to find Ficery.

Ficery was by no means the first—and certainly won't be the last—hiker to walk off into Yosemite's mystery-shrouded forests and mountains to never return. There have been many such incidents and more than a few unfortunate park visitors swallowed up by Yosemite's vast backcountry. Most of these people were likely victims of their own overconfidence and recklessness, and in the majority of these cases, we'll never know exactly what happened to them or why they vanished.

TIOGA PASS ROAD PURCHASED

1915

A dedication marker on the Tioga Pass Road reads: THIS TABLET COMMEMORATES THE SUCCESSFUL LABORS OF STEPHEN T. MATHER, DIRECTOR OF THE NATIONAL PARK SERVICE, IN SECURING FOR THE PEOPLE THE TIOGA PASS ROAD.

That's about as uninteresting a historical marker as one is likely to find out along the nation's highways, but it is far more meaningful than it seems. Motorists who read this dedication marker today likely shrug their shoulders and drive on to enjoy the many attractions of Yosemite National Park. Likely they have never heard of Stephen T. Mather and may only vaguely understand the significance of his accomplishments. One of those accomplishments, of course, was the opening of the vital Tioga Pass Road linking Yosemite to points eastward.

That event was officially celebrated at this very spot on July 28, 1915, the twenty-fifth anniversary of the establishment of Yosemite National Park. Sierra Club leaders William Colby and Clair Tappan had arranged for a dedication to mark the opening of the newly public road. By their sides stood Mather, who had wrapped himself in an American flag for the occasion. Mather spoke to a small crowd of well-wishers about federal acquisition of the road and the end of the era of private exploitation of Yosemite's roadways. He urged continued vigilance against what he saw as the "threat of privatization."

The Tioga Pass Road, today a key section of CA 120, running from the eastern border of Yosemite National Park—the nearest town is 5 miles east at Lee Vining, off US 395 near Mono Lake—most of the way to Crane Flat, near the western border, a total of 46 miles. Oddly named, since "Tioga" is an eastern Iroquois word, not Miwok, this two-lane road is open from the spring thaw until autumn snows blanket the high Sierras.

The road itself began as an Indian trail that was expanded to handle wagons when mines were established in the eastern hills in the late 1800s. At Tioga Pass, the road rises to 9,945 feet, the highest crossing in the Sierras in California. But the road was a toll road, owned and operated by the Swift Packing Company and later by its heirs. And this is where one Stephen Mather comes into the picture.

Stephen T. Mather, one of the few who in the nineteenth century could say he was born, raised, and educated in California, made his fortune by taking over the Pacific Coast Borax Company. An avid outdoorsman, he first visited Yosemite when he was ten years old. His love for the natural beauty of the park and the surrounding Sierras came from his regular visits over his lifetime.

In 1914 Mather made a tour of several national parks and was shocked, according to a biographer, by the terrible conditions of these parks, the failure of park management to meet their mandate of wilderness preservation, and the lack of facilities needed to make the parks usable by visitors. The responsibility for running the federal park system, which by that time included fifteen national parks and eighteen national monuments, had been turned over to the General Land Office. However, each park or monument was independently run, and there was almost no centralized funding or long-range planning. What coordination existed within the system pertained only to Yellowstone, Yosemite, and Sequoia, which were maintained and protected by U.S. Army cavalrymen.

When he complained to the Secretary of the Interior Franklin Lane, a fraternity brother from his days at the University of California, Lane wrote back, "Dear Steve, if you don't like the way the national parks are being run, come on down to Washington and run them yourself." So Mather did exactly that, accepting the position of Assistant Secretary of the Interior.

He took no salary, seeing his job as a public service, and he began to organize support for a coordinated mandate and funding base. His strategy was to impress upon Congress and national leaders the economic viability of a tourist-based national park system and yet to garner support of conservation-oriented groups and individuals for the implementation of a management plan that maintained the wilderness.

It was a fine wire that he walked, but the parks were in bad shape and sadly lacking in meaningful federal protection. It was in this unfortunately permissive political environment that San Francisco won approval for its plan to expropriate much of the Hetch Hetchy canyon for use as a reservoir. However, Mather had a different vision for the nation's park system. He wanted to encourage increased use of these resources by tourists.

In an effort to draw more people to the parks, Mather became focused on issues of accessibility. This was especially important in remote parks like Yosemite, where automobiles had recently appeared for the first time. Meanwhile, Henry Ford and a few of his competitors were promoting inexpensive cars that ordinary workers could afford. Would they use them to visit the nation's parks? Only if there were good roads to make the parks accessible.

The owners of Tioga Pass Road were looking to sell it quickly for a mere $15,500. Mather jumped at the chance. He knew that Congress would take a long time to act, so he offered the owners $7,500 of his own money, a bond of $5,000, and with the help of local county supervisors and donations, the remaining funds were gathered. Congress passed legislation approving the acquisition of the road in 1915.

Only 190 cars came through Tioga Pass that first year, but a lot more were coming. Today, millions of cars enter or pass through Yosemite National Park each year. More than half a million of those take the Tioga Pass Road. They pay no tolls because the American people, rather than some private company, own the road.

Stephen Mather never tired of reminding his fellow citizens of the importance of maintaining the integrity and vitality of the nation's parks. In 1916 he drafted legislation to establish the National Park Service and soon afterward was named its first director. The Act stated that the purpose of the Service is to:

> *promote and regulate the use of the Federal areas*
> *known as national parks, monuments, and reservations*
> *. . . to conserve the scenery and the natural and historic*
> *objects and the wild life therein, and to provide for*
> *the enjoyment of the same in such manner and by such*
> *means as will leave them unimpaired for the enjoyment*
> *of future generations.*

ANSEL ADAMS'S FIRST PHOTOGRAPH

1916

On a warm day during the summer of 1916, a fifteen-year-old boy wandered along a trail near the west end of Yosemite Valley. Likely, he could hear the play of the Merced River as it swept over rocks at the edge of a nearby forest of Douglas fir. He had an ear for music and, as he was about to prove, an eye for art, especially artwork of the variety created by nature.

Up ahead of him, framed by the firs, one of nature's greatest monuments soared skyward. It was El Capitan, and the boy had decided to catch a bit of the rock's magnificent spirit and carry it away with him. The tool he would use for this ambitious project was an ordinary box camera. He was not the first boy to bring a camera to Yosemite and try it out on El Capitan, and he would not be the last, but the photograph he took that day was something quite extraordinary. Perhaps that is because he was Ansel Adams.

Of course, at the age of fifteen, Ansel Adams did not yet know that his name would become known all over the world. In fact, his life up until that moment had not necessarily shown a great deal of promise. Born into a wealthy San Francisco family in 1902, he survived the great earthquake and fire that leveled much of the city when he was just four years old. Perhaps traumatized by this experience, Adams showed early symptoms of severe hyperactivity, a condition that would make it difficult for him to succeed in school. For the same reason he had few friends as a child and rarely, if ever, participated in sports. After young Ansel was dismissed from several private schools because of his inattentive and hyperactive behavior, his family hired private tutors. Adams's formal education, acquired mostly at home, probably did not extend beyond the eighth grade.

Adams demonstrated considerable aptitude for music, however, and his father taught him to play the piano. The boy loved the instrument and poured his restless energy into mastering it. Surprisingly, the discipline that Adams seemed to lack in other areas of education quickly emerged when he sat down in front of a piano keyboard. He quickly learned to play sophisticated classical scores, and the rigorous practice regimen this required seemed to calm him. A large portion of Adams's subsequent life would be devoted to a mostly unsuccessful effort to become a concert pianist.

As it turned out, Adams's artistic talents were not limited to music, at least not of the sort that is heard in concert halls. He saw art in rocks, streams, trees, and clouds—in the infinitely varied shapes and forms of nature. His family had taught him to enjoy the outdoors, to respect nature, and to love natural beauty. The simple box camera his father gave him—and many later more sophisticated and capable cameras—would offer him the opportunity to explore these interests.

Adams's first photograph of El Capitan, the one he took with his box camera, framed the rock with tree limbs that seemed to set it apart from all the rest of nature. The picture emphasized the immense height of the cliff, which appeared bathed in a light that came not just from the sun but from within. It would be just this type of visual insight that would lift Adams to prominence in the world of photographic art.

In a photography career that would span the better part of seven decades, Adams used Yosemite as the focus of many, if not most, of his most famous photographs. It was, in fact, his favorite place in all the world. He saw Yosemite Valley and the surrounding cliffs and mountains in much the way John Muir had seen them—as nature's cathedral. Adams enshrined Yosemite's spectacular scenery with his mostly black-and-white images.

Speaking of his first trip to California's best-known national park, Adams said, "Yosemite burst upon us and it was glorious. There was light everywhere, and seeing it, a new era opened for me."

Adams's link to Yosemite would eventually take on an even more personal dimension. During his frequent visits to the park, he befriended the artist Harry Best, who owned a well-known valley studio. Best allowed Adams to practice on an old piano he kept at the studio. While practicing at Best's studio, Adams met the artist's attractive daughter Virginia, and the two were married in 1928. Ansel and Virginia Adams took over the studio when Harry Best died in 1935. The Best Studio in Yosemite would remain a base of operations for the photographer for the remainder of his career, which lasted another half century.

Adams found that he did not have to wander far from the Best Studio to find suitable subjects for his work. Over the years he photographed El Capitan, Half Dome, and other iconic park features hundreds, if not thousands, of times—at the height of summer, in the snow, in the first flush of spring, and when the last fall leaves clung to the limbs of deciduous trees down along the Merced River. Some of the pictures Adams produced in Yosemite rank among the most famous photographs ever taken.

Adams loved hiking and camping, and he had joined the Sierra Club at the age of seventeen. Over the years, Adams and his work became closely linked to the club and its conservationist causes. Adams is especially well-known for his successful effort to have Kings Canyon set aside as a national park. Located adjacent to Sequoia National Park about 100 miles southeast of Yosemite, Kings Canyon became a national park in 1940.

"I believe in beauty," said Adams. "I believe in stones and water, air and soil, people and their future and their fate."

Adams's philosophical underpinnings, nurtured by childhood camping trips taken with his family, deeply influenced his work as a photographer. Adams often worked with Polaroid film, which allowed him to draw sharp contrasts between towering rocks, clouds, and open sky and heightened the viewer's awareness of the beauty inherent in nature. Adams died in 1984, by which time he had published dozens of books and major collections of his work and become, perhaps, the most famous photographer in the world. Strangely enough, the roots of his career can be traced back to a single Yosemite afternoon in 1916 when he held a simple box camera in his hand and gazed up at El Capitan.

DROWNING A NATIONAL TREASURE

1923

Most of the tourists who visit Yosemite during the summer gaze in wonder at its spectacular beauty and imagine that there must never have been another place like this on the planet. They are wrong, for there once existed not just one but two such valleys in the California Sierra. The first, of course, is Yosemite itself. The other was Hetch Hetchy, a glacial valley a couple of dozen miles to the north. According to all who were lucky enough to see it in its original state, Hetch Hetchy was in nearly every way the equal of Yosemite—in beauty, in grandeur, and in its ability to nurture the human spirit. Unfortunately, the Hetch Hetchy that once rivaled the magnificence of Yosemite is no more. It has been drowned under a reservoir several miles long and up to half a mile wide.

The destruction of Hetch Hetchy had begun years before July 7, 1923, the day on which Michael O'Shaughnessey, a noted civil engineer, stood before a crowd of well-wishers and politicians to dedicate the 227-foot-high dam that would create the Hetch Hetchy Reservoir. By that time, much of the natural beauty that had previously graced the Hetch Hetchy Valley had vanished. The once nearly pristine canyon above the dam had already been denuded of trees and other foliage and its bottom scraped bare to receive the reservoir waters. Now that the dam spillways were closed, a large mountain lake would begin to form and complete the valley's ruin.

The dam, which would later be raised in height to more than 300 feet, would be named after O'Shaughnessey, an appropriate gesture since he had designed it and managed its construction. The dam would eventually hold back 360,000 acre-feet of crystal clear water. O'Shaughnessey had also designed the vast delivery system that would move that high-quality water from the reservoir, across the California Central Valley, and into the spigots of consumers in San Francisco and nearby communities. Certainly with its hundreds of thousands of residents, the bay area was thirsty, but there are those who say it might have gotten the water it needed in any number of ways. There are many who believed then, and others who continue to believe to this day, that Hetch Hetchy need not have been sacrificed.

The drowning of Hetch Hetchy, and along with it the destruction of one of America's greatest natural wonders, took place despite the combative opposition of conservationists the likes of John Muir and of the Sierra Club he helped found. It took place despite the fact that the water really wasn't needed at the time and wouldn't be for decades afterward. It took place despite the fact that there were other sources of water that might have served just as well. How did this happen?

The isolated Hetch Hetchy Valley, a near twin of Yosemite Valley to its south, sits at an elevation of 3,800 feet, about a third of the way up the Sierra Nevada peaks that surround it. The valley in 1900 was filled with thriving pine and oak forests and grassy meadows alive with wildflowers. It was a haven from the heat of the Central Valley to the west and the cold of the 10,000-foot mountain passes to the east.

For much of the last few thousand years, the only humans who regularly visited the Hetch Hetchy were members of the Paiute and Central Miwok tribes, who arrived each summer and fall to hunt. They had long ago altered the landscape by setting fires to clear the land, bring more wildlife to the area to graze, and improve the prospects for hunting. These fires left in their wake a wonderland of open meadows broken here and there by clusters of black oaks that produced tasty acorns relished by the native Indians. Then, during the 1850s came prospectors who also changed the landscape. They scarred the valley rocks here and there digging for gold, silver, and other minerals but otherwise left the land intact.

According to Tenaya, the last chief of the Ahwaneechees, the canyon was called Hetch Hetchy because of a pair of yellow pine trees that once marked its entrance. Tenaya explained that in the Miwok language, "Hetchy" means tree, so "Hetch Hetchy" meant the two trees, or the "Valley of the Two Trees." Others say the valley was named for a type of grass that grows in abundance there and produces edible seeds. Regardless of how it got its interesting name, the valley was treasured by Native Americans and others who visited it right up until the twentieth century.

What may have doomed the Hetch Hetchy was its relative isolation. During the early days of Yosemite tourism and throughout the early history of Yosemite National Park, the Hetch Hetchy had far fewer visitors than did the Yosemite Valley. So when politicians and engineers came looking for a place to build a reservoir, there were not as many citizens prepared to come to its defense as there might have been if Yosemite Valley itself had been at risk.

About the time of the great 1906 earthquake and fire, the city of San Francisco developed a plan to quench the thirst of its growing population. In 1906 the city's population had reached 450,000. Within twenty years it would hit 600,000. Today the population of the entire bay area is approximately 2.4 million. To meet the city's water needs and those of future generations, San Francisco's political leaders looked to the Sierra. There they identified the Tuolumne River as the most likely source of a reliable municipal water supply. To store the river's abundant waters, they needed a reservoir, and the handiest place for it was a glacial valley located within the boundaries of Yosemite National Park—the Hetch Hetchy.

Naturally enough, conservationists threw whatever political obstacles they could in the path of the dam builders. John Muir and others wrote a steady stream of letters to congressmen. They protested vigorously in print and in open meetings, but their efforts were all to no avail. The public was not with them. A century ago, the eyes and hearts of most Americans—Californians especially—were firmly fixed on growth and development. It seemed to them that nature had been put in place for people to use in any way they desired. For the nature lovers of the world, a few scattered parks could be set aside so they could go hiking and take photographs to their hearts' content. Why, after all, they argued, did America need two Yosemites?

What many did not understand was that Hetch Hetchy was, in fact, part of Yosemite National Park, and construction of the O'Shaughnessey Dam caused lasting damage to it. By the time of the 1923 dedication ceremony, the western part of the national park had already suffered extensive damage. Construction and development had scarred not only Hetch Hetchy but also other areas in and near Yosemite. Roads had been blasted out of solid rock. More than 67 miles of track had been laid for a railroad to transport men and construction materials into the valley. And another, smaller reservoir known as Lake Eleanor was created to provide power for construction of the O'Shaughnessey Dam. A small city was built to house and feed the workers, and along with them came the usual mounds of trash, erosion, and environmental degradation.

However, the greatest destruction was the denuding of Hetch Hetchy Valley itself in preparation for its flooding. O'Shaughnessey had hired a contractor to clear the 880-acre floor of trees, which were then sold for lumber. Pictures of Hetch Hetchy after the clearing but before the valley was flooded show a naked land with a black Tuolumne River running through it.

The irony of the demise of the Hetch Hetchy Valley was that for years to come, the San Francisco area did not need the water. In 1915 the city and surrounding communities used about 133 million gallons per day, which the Spring Valley Water Company was able to deliver without difficulty. But the new water system would be capable of delivering 400 million gallons per day. This was the amount engineers were estimating the city would need by the year 2000, several generations in the future.

In fact, while the voters of 1909 had approved a bond measure to build the water system, the only construction for delivery were the dams and the electrical transmission lines to carry the power they generated. San Francisco's neighbors in Oakland, Berkeley, and Richmond had backed away from a potential partnership that would have supplied more funds to the project. Short on money, O'Shaughnessey and his construction crews left the aqueduct, pipes, and tunnels needed to deliver the Hetch Hetchy waters unfinished. These facilities would not be completed until 1934, when San Francisco finally raised the funds needed to complete the project. By that time, the Hetch Hetchy that conservationists and other nature lovers had treasured had been gone for many years.

John Muir had spent the last years of his life in a losing battle to save the Hetch Hetchy. Some say that losing the struggle broke Muir's great heart and so discouraged him that he lost his will to live. Muir died in 1914, believing correctly that the Hetch Hetchy could not be saved.

At the dam dedication nearly a decade later, O'Shaughnessey had little to say about Muir and the other conservationists who had struggled to stop him. However, he did have quite a bit to say about the beauty of the Hetch Hetchy Valley. In his view, the new lake would only enhance that valley's appearances and make it more attractive to visitors.

> The Dam and Hetch Hetchy Reservoir stand as a refutation to so-called nature lovers who opposed its construction. Here, spreading for 7 miles up the valley, lies a placid lake which is destined to become a magnet to all real nature lovers.

In an urban-rural battle that still rages today, the valley was sacrificed to meet the water and power needs of millions of people and thousands of businesses. In the process, the natural beauty of the Hetch Hetchy Valley was replaced by a different sort of beauty, that of the Hetch Hetchy Reservoir, just as O'Shaughnessey had predicted. Although less popular than Yosemite Valley, hikers, campers, and anglers do use this area extensively, enjoying the lake and the enhanced access it provides to the upper part of the Hetch Hetchy canyon. Even so, there are still those who lament the loss of the grand valley the lake has drowned. There are even calls—some quite serious—for dismantling the dam and draining the lake. The idea is to return the Hetch Hetchy to its natural state. That may seem impossible, but who knows the true depth of nature's power to heal?

PRESIDENT KENNEDY'S
GHOSTLY ROCKING CHAIR

1962

Yosemite has rarely seen an entourage as impressive as the one that arrived at the Ahwahnee Hotel on the afternoon of Friday, August 17, 1962. It included a host of personal aides, political advisors, and shifty-eyed Secret Service agents on hand to protect and assist the most important guest to check into the Ahwahnee in many a year. That guest was President John Fitzgerald Kennedy, who was making a quick stopover in Yosemite after a whirlwind political tour of the Midwest and West.

Kennedy's trip had included visits to South Dakota, where he attended a campaign rally for fellow Democrat George McGovern, then running for his first term in the United States Senate, to Pueblo, Colorado, where he celebrated the approval of a major water reclamation project, and elsewhere. The president was working hard to build a stronger majority in Congress to help him get his programs passed. So by the time Kennedy reached California, he was tired and very much in need of a rest.

That is just what Kennedy had hoped his stay at the Ahwahnee would be—restful. However, he had only one night and one morning to spend relaxing amid the towering cliffs, waterfalls, and other scenic splendors of Yosemite National Park. Afterwards, he would be off to do another day's campaigning in California and to join his sister Patricia and her husband, Peter Lawford, for a brief visit in their Santa Monica home.

Although Kennedy was weary from travel and constant campaigning, his trademark charm was very much in evidence as he entered the Ahwahnee with his aides and Secret Service guards trailing along behind. He greeted everyone—hotel managers, bellhops, chefs, waiters, drivers, and other guests—warmly and shook every hand that was extended toward him. Then he retired to the third floor, which had been reserved in its entirety for the president and others in his party. A special piece of furniture had been installed in the presidential suite, and no doubt, Kennedy was looking forward to settling into it. The Ahwahnee management had located a rocking chair much like the one Kennedy used at the White House and had it placed in his sitting room. Kennedy had a bad back, so the room was also outfitted with a special orthopedic mattress.

Perhaps the biggest accommodation made for the president at Ahwahnee was in the hotel telephone switchboard. It was temporarily replaced by a fully operational replica of the official presidential switchboard at the White House in Washington. Of course, there were no cell phones or laptop computers in those days, and it was vitally important for the president to remain in touch with members of his cabinet and with the commanders of the various armed services. It was impossible to tell when some freak accident or ill-considered decision on the part of one or another world leader might push the nation and the planet to the brink of war—possibly even a nuclear war. As a matter of fact, at just this moment tensions were rising in

Berlin, where U.S. and Soviet forces kept a wary eye on one another from either side of the now infamous Berlin Wall. It seemed likely that a superpower showdown might come at any moment. Indeed, just such a confrontation between the nuclear-armed nations would come only two months later during the Cuban Missile Crisis.

Fortunately, the only fireworks that held Kennedy's attention during his stay in Yosemite was the Glacier Point Firefall performance, which in those days was held each night at 9:00. The president had expressed special interest in seeing it, but as it turned out, the evening event he attended in the Ahwahnee dining room ran late. An expert fisherman had been assigned especially to catch fresh local trout for the president, so Kennedy may have been lingering over the remains of an especially tasty dinner. Rather than disappoint the chief executive—after all, he was their boss—the rangers responsible for the Firefall waited until the president had finished eating and made it outside to see the show. Unaware of the reason for the delay, tourists in parking lots around the park started blowing their horns as if they were at a drive-in theater with a broken projector. Although it started about thirty minutes late, the Firefall proved an especially beautiful one, much to the delight of President Kennedy and his fellow spectators.

Kennedy praised the spectacle, the Ahwahnee, and Yosemite in general when he addressed a crowd of local residents and park rangers before he left on Saturday. "You have a beautiful park here, and you keep it up beautifully," said the president. "I am sure that all Americans who come here will feel better, not only about the National Park Service but also about their country."

Kennedy's support for the national park system is well documented, although it is impossible to say how much of that was due to his enjoyable stay at Yosemite in 1962. However, it is pleasing to imagine the young president—he was only forty-five years old at the time—rocking in his chair at the Ahwahnee and considering the importance of preserving scenic treasures such as Yosemite. As Kennedy often said in speeches, people need frequent exposure to the out-of-doors and to nature.

Some workers and guests at the Ahwahnee have had no trouble at all imagining President Kennedy in his rocking chair. That is because during the years since Kennedy's visit to Yosemite and his tragic death in 1963 in Dallas, more than a few claim to have heard the chair rocking back and forth in the night. There are no rocking chairs in the guest rooms at the Ahwahnee. The Kennedy chair was removed soon after he left the hotel in 1962. Even so, more than a few hotel workers claim to have seen it when they cleaned the rooms he occupied that August. When hotel managers check to see for themselves, the rocking chair is always gone.

SWEPT OVER THE FALLS

1970

June 18, 1970, was an unusually warm day in Yosemite, so perhaps it is easy to understand why people would want to splash around in the cooling waters of the Merced River. Wading in the river as it coursed sluggishly along the valley floor would likely have been harmless enough. However, stepping into the river only a few yards from the edge of Vernal Falls could lead to tragedy. In fact, it did for a thirty-year-old La Peunte, California, mother and her nine-year old daughter.

Yolanda Fuentes and her young daughter, Christine, were enjoying what had been a delightful Yosemite outing with several relatives. The Mist Trail that runs below Grizzly Peak and the Panorama Cliffs was as inviting then as it is today, and the Fuentes family decided to go for a hike. The trail carried them to the top of Vernal Falls, where they stopped to admire the view and watch the river water slip over the brink and disappear into the valley below.

Perhaps because they were hot and sweaty from their hike—no one has ever been quite sure why—the family decided to climb over the guard rails and dip their toes in the river. The guardrails had warning signs, but these were ignored or they were not understood. The river here was deceptively docile and flowed unthreatening over the rocks in its channel just as it did in the valley below. It was likely hard for anyone in the family to comprehend the danger. Unfortunately, the danger was only too real. Only about 20 yards downriver, the Merced's rocky bed was replaced by thin air as its waters plunged into a free fall the length of a football field. Apparently oblivious to this deadly hazard, the mother, her daughter, and several others waded into the Merced, where they laughed, splashed water on one another, or sat on rocks cooling their feet in the rushing water.

Seeing what was happening, a nearby hiker shouted and pointed at the warning signs. "The railing was put there to keep kids from going over the falls," he said. Apparently, no one listened.

About that time, one of the women in the Fuentes party reached for her camera. She intended to take a picture, but the photograph she wanted—of family members having a good time—would never be taken. As she lowered her head to work with the camera settings, her hat fell off into the river. Floating like a leaf on the surface, it began to move along toward the falls, slowly at first and then more quickly.

Christine Fuentes was nearby when the hat plopped into the water, and she scrambled after it into the river. The little girl was small even for her age, and the current readily took hold of her. Crying out and with arms flailing, Christine was carried inexorably toward the fall. Not far behind was her mother Yolanda, who was making a desperate—and as it turned out, fatal—attempt to save her daughter. The hat shot over the fall, followed a split second afterward by Christine. A moment after that Yolanda vanished as well.

Several people, including the other members of the Fuentes party, witnessed this tragedy. They screamed and called out. They ran toward the river, though fortunately not into it. None could do anything to help, and none would ever forget.

It seems almost impossible to imagine that in a place as well-known and heavily traveled as Yosemite that two people could vanish in an instant, but in this case they did. Would-be rescuers and search parties were unable to locate the bodies of either of the victims. More than two months after the incident, the remains of Yolanda Fuentes were finally located. No trace of Christine Fuentes was ever found.

Although people had been swept over Yosemite waterfalls in the past, this was the first such incident in the 1970s, a decade that would prove especially deadly in this respect. There were only four fatal accidents of this kind during the 1960s—there had been none in 1950s—but there were to be no fewer than seventeen fatal waterfall plunges in Yosemite during the 1970s. During three decades since the 1970s, there have been only about a dozen.

No one is sure why Yosemite's waterfalls were so deadly during the 1970s. In fact, the very day after the Fuentes tragedy, teenager Chris Goldman from Davis, California, took a fatal plunge over Staircase Falls. Little more than a month later, Nicholas Cordil of Los Angeles fell over Upper Yosemite Falls. No one witnessed the accident, but it is possible that Cordil fell more than 1,000 feet. His body was recovered in pieces. The deadliest year for Yosemite's waterfalls was 1971, when five people, ranging in age from nine to twenty-two, took a fatal plunge.

Waterfalls are among the most beautiful and dramatic spectacles in nature. Unfortunately, they are also among the most deadly. Yosemite's waterfalls are more dangerous than most.

When people go on hikes in the wilderness or in a park or natural area such as Yosemite, a waterfall is very often their destination. When they reach the waterfall, they may pull out their cameras or spread out a picnic on some convenient rock that offers them a view of the plunging water. That's the safe way to enjoy a waterfall, but there are other ways that are very dangerous indeed. Anyone who gets too near the base of the falls is in danger of being struck by falling rocks or heavy chunks of wood. They also run the risk of being pulled into deep pools and drowned by the swirling water.

Those who approach the waterfall rim above run an even greater risk. They may slip on the rocks and fall over the cliff—an accident that is nearly always fatal. Or, like the unfortunate Christine Fuentes and her mother, they may get caught in the swift-running stream that feeds the falls and swept over the edge. Waterfalls are very lovely and inviting, and it is understandable that people—children especially—want to get close. However, the best policy is to keep a safe and respectable distance. Otherwise, a happy outing may turn suddenly to tragedy.

WAR IN THE VALLEY OF PEACE

1970

Yosemite Valley is always crowded on holidays, and on July 4, 1970, congestion in the park was especially heavy. This was one of the long, hot summers of the Vietnam War period. Richard Nixon was president. He had said he would get America out of the war but had not done so. Young people opposed to the war did not trust him. In fact, they trusted no one in authority, whether that person was a president, a parent, a policeman, or a park ranger. They felt they had good reasons to withhold their trust, believing, as the young often do, that they could reshape the planet and make of it a better, more peaceful world. However, there would be very little peace in Yosemite on this Independence Day.

Early that morning, long lines of automobiles jammed the roads leading into Yosemite Valley. Many of these cars held family picnickers from San Francisco, Sacramento, Oakland, and other northern California cities. However, an unusually large number of these vehicles were packed with high school kids, college students, and other young people who were, as many said at the time, "just being in the now." Often, the young men had long hair and beards and the young women wore flower-print dresses. There were lots of small trucks, buses, and vans painted with fantastic scenes that seemed to have sprung from dreams, either wondrous, nightmarish, or both.

Yosemite park officials and rangers understood only too well that this would be a difficult day. There would be lots of alcohol in the park, and there would most certainly be drugs. There would also be plenty of rowdiness and, no doubt, some public nudity as well. Rangers would attempt to enforce the laws and park regulations as best they could, but no plans were made for a general crackdown. Every available ranger would be on duty throughout the day and into the evening, but their orders as always would be to spend most of their time protecting lives and park property.

Early in the day, large numbers of young revelers had begun to gather in Stoneman Meadow, a broad, grassy area across the road from Curry Village. Frequented by deer and other wildlife, the meadow is one of Yosemite's less obvious, but nonetheless attractive features. During the spring, it is alive with azaleas and in the summer with yarrow and black-eyed Susans. The Merced River and a stand of tall Douglas fir enclose one side of the meadow, and one of the main park access roads lines the other.

By the middle of the day, Stoneman Meadow had become the site of what might be described as an unplanned pop festival. Guitars and other instruments had been pulled out of Volkswagen buses and the trunks of battered cars, and impromptu bands were playing their own versions of Grateful Dead, Rolling Stones, or Led Zeppelin hits. The music had begun to mesmerize the Stoneman Meadow crowd, which seemed to be growing larger by the minute. The audience sat on the ground or on blankets spread over the meadow grasses, drinking, smoking, and thoroughly enjoying themselves. Many of the young listeners were barefooted and more than a few, both male and female, sported bare chests.

Soon the size and general mood of the crowd began to alarm park officials. It has never been clear who, if anyone, decided that the gathering on Stoneman Meadow must be broken up, but by the middle of the afternoon, rangers were posting closure signs and ordering people to leave the area. Their orders were ignored, and their signs were smashed to bits and thrown into the Merced River. Soon, tempers grew short, fights broke out, and rangers called in law enforcement assistance from communities outside the park. Thus began what would eventually be called the Stoneman Meadow Riot, an incident that would be widely reported in newspapers and on newscasts across the country.

Seeing their closure signs floating in pieces down the Merced, rangers and their law enforcement allies used loudspeakers and bullhorns to order everyone away from the meadow. As before, few complied with the order. Exasperated rangers and police then attempted to make arrests but were met with determined resistance. Young protesters started throwing empty liquor and beer bottles at them, and the officers replied by throwing rocks.

"We used to call it the Rock and Bottle Festival," said one ranger who took part in the incident. "The hippies threw bottles and we threw rocks. It had turned into a riot, and unfortunately, more than a few rangers lost their heads and joined in the fighting."

Having completely lost control of the situation, law enforcement officials knew they'd need a major show of force to quell the disturbance. They decided to use mounted riot police. They would once again employ bullhorns to announce closure of the meadow and order people to leave. If they did not leave, mounted rangers and police officers armed with clubs would move in and clear the area.

It may be that the rioters simply didn't know how to comply with the order. Yosemite is a big park, but the valley is a relatively restricted area. Where would they go if they left the meadow, and would they be safe when they got there? Whatever was in the protesters' minds at this point, most stood their ground.

Seeing no response to their order, the mounted rangers and police charged into the crowd swinging their clubs. The protesters fled, but the fighting was not as one-sided as one might think. Police cars parked along the road or in the Curry Village parking area were overturned and some were set on fire. The fighting went on into the night, and there were dozens of injuries and a hundred or more arrests.

For months after the riot, rangers attempted to keep people they identified as "hippies" out of the park. Buses and vans loaded with young campers from San Francisco were often turned away from park entrances on some largely technical pretext. For instance, the ranger might claim that the vehicle appeared unsafe or that one of the occupants of the vehicle appeared to be inebriated. Recognizing that these efforts were likely an illegal infringement of people's rights, rangers eventually gave up trying to keep the park free of flower children.

In time, the Vietnam War ended and so did the era of protests. Even so, there were few who were in Yosemite on July, 4, 1970, who would ever forget the experience. After all, that was the day the valley of peace hosted its very own undeclared war.

CRASH OF
THE *LODESTAR LIGHTNING*

1976

No one knows for sure what the last few minutes of life were like for pilot Jon Glisky and his copilot Jeffrey Nelson, only that they must have been frightening. Both about age thirty and both from Seattle, Glisky and Nelson had taken off from a remote beachside runway somewhere in Baja California. Authorities believe they were headed for another remote runway at Black Rock Desert, about 60 miles northeast of Reno and 50 miles west of Winnemucca, Nevada. Authorities also believe that onboard their plane were several tons of marijuana.

It was December, and Glisky and Nelson were probably looking forward to spending the holidays with friends and family in Seattle. They may also have been looking forward to cashing in on a highly profitable business venture. If fully loaded with 140-pound bales of marijuana, the *Lodestar Lightning* could have carried a cargo worth upwards of $1 million. Unfortunately for the two young men, their airplane never reached its desert airfield in Nevada. It disappeared.

The *Lodestar Lightning* should have been able to make the trip with little trouble. It was a Lockheed PV-1 Ventura, a type of World War II bomber also used occasionally for submarine patrols. The Ventura had been refurbished with two jets that created a total of 5,000 additional horsepower and gave it the ability to fly up to 2,200 miles on a single tank of fuel. Unknown to Glisky and Nelson, however, something was terribly wrong with their airplane.

Apparently, trying to hop across the Sierra and down into the Reno area, Glisky and Nelson throttled up the aging plane's engines. Somewhere over the mountains above Yosemite Valley, one of the engines fell off and the rest of the airplane soon followed it to earth. Pieces of the plane were scattered across the Yosemite Highlands near Merced Pass, but the bulk of the fuselage and its cargo ended up in Lower Merced Pass Lake. No one saw or heard the crash. The airplane and those onboard simply vanished.

Several weeks later, two backcountry hikers made a mysterious discovery in the highlands. They came across the wing of an airplane. Though battered and torn from impact with the ground, the metal wing had not aged much from exposure to the elements. The backpackers correctly surmised that they had found evidence of a recent crash and reported their find to park rangers in Yosemite. By this time, federal drug officials had started looking for the *Lodestar Lightning*. When the airplane went missing, they had learned of its unusual itinerary and reached what seemed to them an obvious conclusion—the airplane had been making a drug-smuggling run.

Within a week Yosemite was alive with drug enforcement agents. Together with a party of Yosemite National Park rangers, they reached Lower Merced Lake by helicopter, where they surveyed the crash site. While temperatures were unusually warm for a Yosemite winter, the lake's waters were frigid, and the 9,000-foot elevation was enough to strain the breathing of even a well-conditioned agent.

Nevertheless, the search was quite thorough and agents cut through the lake ice to allow wetsuit-clad divers to search in the black waters below. In the murky lake waters, now polluted with jet fuel and hydraulic fluid, searchers managed to locate the fuselage but found no bodies. However, plenty of evidence relating to the airplane's illicit cargo was discovered. Over a ton of marijuana was pulled out of the lake. A recovery effort aimed at removing the marijuana from blocks of ice on the surface had netted another thousand pounds of the stuff before an early February blizzard shut down the operation.

By this time, news of the crashed airplane and its cargo had reached the ears of nearly everyone in central California. It did not occur to law enforcement authorities that there were interested parties willing to brave the terrible weather in order to reach the crash site, so it was left unguarded. As it turned out, more than a few fortune hunters made the climb to Lower Merced Pass Lake and were able to reap considerable rewards for their efforts. Down in the valley, wet and oily "Lodestar Lightning" marijuana provided many with a warm buzz that winter.

When authorities returned in the spring, they found the crash site had been tampered with and that valuable evidence had been removed. To stop the pilfering, six armed U.S. Customs agents were air-dropped into the area. The drop surprised a party of hikers searching for marijuana, and when they saw the parachutes open, they made a run for it. Most got away, but the agents managed to arrest two of the young salvagers. Despite the presence of armed guards, several more attempts were made to raid the crash site and make off with marijuana. By the late spring, more than a little of the remaining cargo had disappeared. There was none left at all by summer, when rangers and law officers returned to the lake to finish their work.

With the official recovery effort once more under way, divers returned to the frigid lake waters. Not long afterward, one of them surfaced with the body of Jeffrey Nelson in tow. Jon Glisky's body was located as well. Later, many parts of the submerged plane, including the fuselage, were recovered.

The Justice Department attempted to track down and arrest anyone who had participated in the Glisky/Nelson smuggling operation, which they tied to a dummy corporation in Florida. These efforts proved mostly unsuccessful. However, investigators eventually found that a lawyer in Santa Barbara, California, was the legal owner of the *Lodestar Lightning,* and a bill was presented to him for salvage costs of more than $20,000. The bill has never been paid.

The crash of the *Lodestar Lightning* remains a Yosemite legend to this day. It provides grist for stories told around summer campfires and a reason for some hopeful hikers to visit Lower Merced Pass Lake. Not every story told about the crash is true. Nor are all the stories false.

TRAGEDY STRIKES HALF DOME

1985

Everyone, it seems, wants to climb Half Dome, the sheer arc of stone that is one of the great landmarks of Yosemite National Park. Once believed to be impossible for a human being to climb, Half Dome was finally conquered in 1875 by the inveterate Scots outdoorsman George Anderson. It took Anderson two days of near Herculean exertions to scale the 8,842-foot Dome, which rises as much as 4,000 feet above the valley floor. Nowadays, the task of reaching the top has been made easier by a set of wooden stairs held in place by steel cables. Even so, the ascent takes from four to six hours of steady hiking and covers more than 8 miles.

Despite the difficulty of the climb, thousands of sturdy hikers now attempt the ascent of Half Dome each year. There are times, however, when no one should set foot on the mountain. In Yosemite, as elsewhere in the outdoors when common sense is ignored, tragedy is often the result. This is the story of one such occasion.

It was July 1985, and storms had been rolling through the Sierras all summer long. Yosemite's afternoons had been filled with rain, lightning, and thunder for days, but this did not deter Robert Firth and four of his hiking buddies, who were determined to challenge Half Dome. As they approached the foot of Half Dome in preparation for their climb, they ignored the signs clearly warning all hikers to turn around and seek safe shelter if there are electrical storms in the area. In fact, Firth's group had originally included nine hikers, but four of them had reached the conclusion that it was just too dangerous to climb that day and had walked back down the mountain to the safety of the valley below. The other five—Firth, twenty-four; Adrian Esteban, twenty-seven; Thomas Rice, twenty-eight; Bruce Weiner, twenty-four; and Brian Jordan, sixteen—would soon experience the most terrifying adventure of their lives.

As the five remaining hikers set off for the summit, they could already hear the rumble of distant thunder. Starting out from the Happy Isles Trailhead, they carried full packs and sleeping bags since they planned to spend the night either near the Half Dome summit or somewhere along the trail. They had not gone far before rain began to fall, but determined to reach the top, they decided to continue. This decision would prove to have been a terrible mistake.

By the time the hikers reached the crest of the dome, they found themselves caught in a torrential downpour. Seeking shelter from the rain, they clambered under the cleft of a rock overhanging the northwest face of the dome, the side most often seen in photos. This would prove to have been yet another mistake. Like most Yosemite storms, this one had blown in from the west, and the hikers' supposed refuge faced that direction, exposing them to the full fury of the tempest.

Fascinated by the lightning, Firth sat on the edge of the cliff, dangling his feet over the precipice. Not so bold as Firth, the others huddled against the massive wall of stone, hoping the storm would soon pass so that they could climb down in safety. Unfortunately, on this day, safety was beyond their reach.

A bolt of lightning struck the dome and skipped directly into the crevice where Jordan, Rice, Weiner, and Esteban had gathered. Jordan died instantly, while Rice and Weiner were each severely burned. Esteban, who was clinging to the granite, received somewhat less severe burns on his legs and buttocks but was left numb and barely able to move for as much as a quarter of an hour.

Even more exposed than his four companions, Firth had been struck in the head. The bolt left him delirious, vomiting, and speaking gibberish. Wracked by convulsions, he writhed on the ground precariously close to the edge of the cliff, while his injured friends struggled desperately to restrain him and prevent him from falling over the edge.

Lightning continued to strike all around, and a second bolt hit nearby, but this time none of the five climbers were struck. Meanwhile, Firth continued to roll this way and that. Esteban, who had recovered his senses and the use of his limbs, reached out to Firth, grabbing his shirt. Then the shirt began to part, ripping a little at first and then more as Firth's weight pulled it from Esteban's grasp. Almost in slow motion the tragedy unfolded as Firth at last broke free, rolled over one more time, and fell to his death.

Too badly injured to hike and too frightened to leave their refuge, the survivors imagined they would soon join their lost companions in death. Since there was no means of communicating with potential rescuers in Yosemite Valley far below, they started shouting in the hopes that someone would hear them. Fortunately, two teenage hikers finally heard their calls. The two young hikers then headed back down the mountain to seek help. It took them nearly three hours to reach a ranger station, but soon after they raised the alarm, a helicopter was on its way to Half Dome for a daring moonlight rescue.

While the teenagers were climbing down, two female paramedics happened to be climbing on a lower trail, heard the cries of the injured hikers on Half Dome, and went to their assistance. The two women removed the men's clothes and wrapped them in their sleeping bags. Then they waited for help.

About midnight, as the moon began to set, a medical helicopter arrived from Modesto. Flying in the uncertain currents of Yosemite's peaks and valleys is always dangerous, but even more so on that night, as three separate trips were required to pluck the young men from the mountain. Fortunately, the mission proceeded without incident, and by 1:00 a.m. it was over. Esteban was treated and then released from the Yosemite clinic, while Weiner and Rice were flown to Sacramento for surgery to deal with their burns. The bodies of Jordan and Firth were found and evacuated the following day. Afterward, Yosemite rangers decided to close the Half Dome summit, much to the consternation of eager hikers seeking a once-in-a-lifetime experience.

PARAPLEGIC CONQUERS
EL CAPITAN

1989

On a bright July morning in 1989, Marc Wellman looked up at the 3,000-foot granite cliff of El Capitan in Yosemite and saw in it the challenge of a lifetime. He would not be the first rock climber to do so nor the last, but his climb, if he accomplished it, would certainly be a first. Wellman was a paraplegic.

In 1982 Wellman had lost the use of his legs in a mountaineering accident, when he fell approximately 100 feet off Seven Gables in the John Muir Wilderness, but he never gave up his dream of reaching great heights. Rolling in his wheelchair through the halls of West Valley College in Saratoga, he took special courses that qualified him for a Park Management certificate and a job in Yosemite working as an interpretive ranger and director of a disabled access services program.

Despite his accident, Wellman never lost his fascination with mountaineering. From the age of twelve, he had been an inveterate rock climber and had made many difficult ascents, but his fall had seemingly relegated him to the role of an interested observer. Then, in 1989 Wellman saw a news story about a man who had been dragged up a mountain in a wheelchair. This inspired him to reenter the sport as an active participant, but Wellman did not want to be dragged up a cliff face. If he was going to climb, he wanted to do it using his own muscles. So, with the help of a mountain-climbing friend, Wellman developed a technique that would allow him to pull himself up under his own power. For his first big climb, he set his sights on El Capitan, the stellar Yosemite landmark known to rock climbers the world over.

Climbing El Capitan is a tremendous challenge even without the limitations of not having the use of one's legs. It was once thought that the mountain's nearly vertical granite face could not be climbed at all, but improvements in climbing techniques and equipment finally made an ascent possible. On July 4, 1957, Warren Harding and several friends began a grueling assault on the El Capitan summit that would make them the first climbers to reach the top. To accomplish this they designed specially forged pitons and bolts and devised a strategy known as "siege climbing" that would later be used to scale the great peaks of the Himalayas. Harding and his associates identified six ledges that would be their initial goals. Upon reaching each ledge, they would return to the previous landing and haul up water, food, and equipment before climbing on to the next ledge. This technique allowed them to replenish their supplies for each new leg of the climb. It also allowed them to spread their adventure out over nearly sixteen months, during which time they actually climbed only forty-seven days.

When climbing, Harding and the others used highly specialized equipment. Where there were no natural cracks into which a piton could go, they hammered bolts into the rock, a process that scarred the face of the mountain. They were later criticized for this by those who felt that climbers should find natural routes and not damage mountains while they climbed. In all, they used 675 pitons and 125 bolts to complete their climb. Afterward, Harding said he wasn't sure whether they had conquered El Capitan or it had conquered them. "I do recall that El Cap seemed to be in much better condition than I was," said Harding.

Just as Harding had more than thirty years earlier, Marc Wellman understood that "conquering" El Capitan was not an option. He just wanted to climb it, and to make his seemingly impossible dream a reality, he would have to do what Harding and his friends had done—invent a new way to ascend the cliff face. With the help of his good friend Mike Corbett, who held the record at the time of forty-one climbs of El Capitan, Wellman devised a climbing method that might just work. Climbing together, Corbett would affix the pitons and ropes and Wellman would pull himself up. In a few especially difficult parts of the climb, it would be necessary for Corbett to carry his friend on this back, but most of the time Wellman would do the work himself.

The two friends repeatedly practiced their climbing technique on lesser obstacles but could not be sure that it would take them all the way to the top of El Capitan. After all, this climb would require much more than manhandling themselves to the top. Corbett and Wellman expected their El Capitan climb to take at least six days, so they would have to carry along 200 pounds of food and water, as well as climbing gear and hammocks for sleeping. Could they manage it?

"One thing I agreed with him from the start," Corbett said. "I wouldn't pull him."

As the day for the start of the big climb approached, Wellman felt he was ready. He had kept himself in good shape through constant exercise and was able to bench press 240 pounds. He also skied and swam.

"I just wanted to blast off," Wellman said.

Finally, on Wednesday, July 20, the time had come to climb. Wearing foam-padded chaps to protect his legs from chafing and using specially designed rope clamps called "jumars," Wellman started up the El Capitan cliff face accompanied by his friend. Using a method of climbing called "multi-pitch," where several lengths of rope are used to move upward, Corbett would scale a 125-foot length of the cliff to set the pitons and the ropes, while Wellman would pull himself up using jumar clamps. Once at the top of the rope, Wellman then would disconnect from the rope so that Corbett could use it for the next leg of the ascent. Wellman has estimated that he made over 7,000 pull-ups to complete the journey. At night, the climbers rested in their hammocks, which were hung from the side of the sheer cliff.

The climb went slower than expected, due mostly to the winds, which at times pushed the climbers as much as 10 feet away from the cliff. The weather was hot, and this drained their energy. After six days, they had still not reached the top, but by the end of the seventh day Wellman and Corbett had at last reached the famous El Capitan "Nose." This was the same 40-foot outcropping Harding and his friends had first grappled with more than thirty-one years earlier. Their last night on the mountain, the climbers slept on Chickenhead Ledge, just 300 feet from the summit.

When they woke the following morning, the two men weren't sure they had the strength to make the final ascent. However, leaving all their unneeded gear behind, they made the attempt. A few hours later, carrying Wellman piggyback, Corbett finished his forty-second climb and Wellman finished his first. It was done.

During the years since his El Capitan climb, there have been many who have praised Wellman for his feat. There have also been those who, for various reasons, have criticized it. Wellman himself says he hopes his achievement will motivate others to accomplish things that were once only dreams.

"If you feel you can do it, just go for it," said Wellman. "That's what it's all about."

FIRESTORM AT FORESTA

1990

Deep in Yosemite Valley is the village of Foresta, a group of about seventy-five cabins hidden away in the trees. Dating back to the 1800s, Foresta was once a summer home community where children spent time hiking, playing in the forest, and learning about nature, but in a few short hours on a hot, dry August day in 1990, Foresta would be turned to ash in a mighty conflagration. The fiery destruction was touched off, not by a match but by lightning—a virtual wall of lightning, in fact.

California had been aflame since August 3, when lightning strikes in various parts of the state started massive blazes that would eventually consume tens of thousands of acres. Until August 10, however, Yosemite had been untouched by the destruction, and thousands of visitors continued to enjoy the splendors of the park. Certainly Yosemite, which was celebrating its centennial, had seen more than its share of forest fires over the years, but nothing to match what hit the park on this windswept day. Early in the afternoon, dark clouds began to cluster around the Yosemite peaks, and very soon lightning started striking trees here and there in the 860,000-acre park. As many as fifty-five lightning strikes were observed during a relatively short four-hour period, and these started twenty-eight separate fires.

Firefighting crews throughout California were already strained and exhausted, and their equipment thinly spread, when the dry floor of Yosemite Valley caught fire. Foresta residents, along with 10,000 park visitors, had to be evacuated as the Arch Rock Fire took off, producing a firestorm that threatened the cabins of Foresta and other small communities in and around Yosemite. Before it was all over, firefighters and equipment from around the nation would be ferried in by road and helicopter to save Yosemite itself, one of the nation's priceless treasures, from destruction.

Getting visitors safely out of Yosemite proved difficult. On the first day of the crisis, several thousand day visitors became trapped inside the park as the fire jumped across access roads or burned the scrub along hillsides, causing rockslides. Unable to get out, many visitors had to spend an anxious night with raging fires lighting up the sky just miles away. Finally, on the following day, park rangers and firefighters managed to open the roads so that park visitors could escape.

With the visitors safely out of Yosemite and the park entrances officially closed, firefighters and park personnel could concentrate on halting the advancing wall of flame. Overworked, understaffed, and underequipped, fire crews put up a valiant fight, but the fires proved extremely difficult to contain. Temperatures hovered around 100 degrees, while dry winds blew flaming embers across fire lines. The density of the forest and the rough terrain made it nearly impossible to surround and contain fires before they had time to spread else-where. Even so, most of the wildfires were brought under control, but three continued to spread at an alarming rate.

A National Park Service policy, established after a 1920s fire in Yellowstone National Park destroyed 80 square miles of forest, directed rangers and firefighters to suppress all fires. This policy had the unexpected consequence of allowing large amounts of fuel to build up on the forest floor and create conditions ripe for a calamitous forest fire. Under ordinary circumstances, this fuel might have been consumed over the years by a series of small fires that caused relatively little destruction. Eventually, this policy was reversed and some fires were allowed to burn. In some cases, prescribed fires were actually set in order to burn away excess fuel. To some extent this was done in Yosemite, but in many places throughout the park, a 2-foot-deep layer of dead timbers and undergrowth had built up, increasing the likelihood of a highly destructive crown fire, which spreads through the treetops instead of along the ground. This is the type of blaze Yosemite firefighters faced in 1990.

Foresta, and the western part of the park, had no chance as the fire roared through, producing a 300-foot-high wall of flame and a 5-mile-high smoke plume. Firefighters made a desperate stand, establishing a defensive fire line just outside Foresta, but it could not be held. Soon a great ball of flame broke through the line, forcing the firefighters to retreat once again. Now defenseless, the little community was quickly turned to ash. Among the structures lost was the home of Yosemite's historian, Shirley Sargent, whose priceless collection of books and artifacts could not be saved.

It took more than a week to bring the largest Yosemite fires under control, and by that time 24,000 acres had been scorched. Even so, the park was able to reopen on August 17, and within a month or two, visitors began to notice one of nature's most exquisite phenomena: the process of rebirth. Across much of the burned-over area sprouted the rarely seen harlequin lupine. Wildflowers such as the lupine flourish in the sunlight and rich soils left behind when fires clear away trees and debris. In many places oaks began to take root since the great heat of the fire had burst the hard shells of acorns, spilling the seeds they contained into the freshly fertilized soil. The burned fields and forests were springing back to life.

And what of Foresta, the little cabin community destroyed in the fire? The owners wanted to rebuild, but the Park Service denied them permits because of septic problems. Undeterred, some residents turned to the legal system; when they failed in the courts, they appealed directly to the Secretary of the Interior, Manuel Lujan. In the end, Lujan countermanded the Park Service decision, allowing the owners to rebuild. However, most did not return. The natural beauty that attracted them to Foresta in the first place had vanished and been replaced by a charred forest. It will take decades yet for this part of the Yosemite to recover; meanwhile, former Foresta residents have only their memories to cherish.

CAMPERS
VERSUS BEARS

1996

Kira Juliusson wasn't a tourist and wasn't on a hike when the bear attacked her. In fact, the twenty-year-old was a summer Yosemite National Park employee, and she was walking with some friends near the dormitory-like residence she shared with other park workers. It was a warm late August day in 1996, and perhaps lost in her thoughts, Juliusson became separated from her companions. Then, while passing some bear-proof food lockers often used by Yosemite Valley campers, she was accosted by a sizeable brown bear.

Having come face to face with an animal more than twice her size and capable of tearing a human being apart, she might have been terrified, but what she felt instead of terror was mostly shock. Although Yosemite is a nature park, in fact, one of the best-known such places in the world, it can seem a very civilized place. There are hotels, restaurants, grocery stores, snack bars, and in the summer, lots and lots of cars and people. Confronting an aggressive and possibly deadly beast in Yosemite, with strolling tourists eating ice-cream cones half a block away, can seem every bit as unexpected as being bitten by a timber rattler in one's own backyard.

The bear may have been no less startled than Juliusson. It is impossible to say why it reacted as it did. Likely it was frightened. In response to its sudden chance encounter with a human, it reacted more or less predictably. It bit her on the forearm and then ran for its life—in vain, as things turned out.

Juliusson's screams brought her friends quickly to her side. Seeing that she was injured, they hurried her off to a national park clinic, where she received a rabies test and seven stitches to close the wound made by the bear's bite. They also reported the incident to rangers, who now had an unhappy duty to perform.

Rangers were relatively certain that the bear was no true menace to park tourists or employees. They figured it had been searching for food when it ran unexpectedly into Juliusson and fought back in what it thought was self-defense. Nonetheless, public policy required them to track down the unfortunate bear and kill it.

Encounters with humans in Yosemite and elsewhere more often than not turn out much worse for bears than for the people they injure or just frighten. In the entire history of Yosemite, there has not been a single confirmed report of a fatal bear attack on a human. During the last century, there have been only a few such attacks in the entire United States. However, some of these have occurred in Yellowstone and Glacier National Parks, places where grizzlies and other bears often come into close contact with people.

Yosemite visitors and employees occasionally see bears on the side of the road, out along trails, and even in campgrounds and other often-crowded public facilities. Park rangers make every effort to keep bears away from populated areas in the park. At times, however, bears and people inevitably get much closer to one another than they should for safety's sake. But as was the case in the 1996 Juliusson incident, such an encounter is much more likely to be disastrous for the bear than the people.

Coincidentally, just a few days before Juliusson's injury, a group of Yosemite campers had actually attacked and killed a small bear that was apparently doing them no harm. According to San Francisco newspapers, a group of young campers from Orange County, California, had hiked with two chaperones into the backcountry of Little Yosemite Valley. There they were surprised by a two-year-old black bear wandering near their campsite. Witnesses camping nearby reported that several of the young people approached the bear and started throwing stones at it. The bear was first injured by the stones and then took a fatal hit in the head. Park rangers who investigated the incident said it appeared that the bear had not been accidentally struck, but rather had been intentionally stoned to death. Rangers said there also did not appear to have been a reasonable motive for the attack on the bear. The animal, which weighed only about 100 pounds, was not menacing anyone.

No arrests were made, but park rangers and officials took a very dim view of the killing. Investigators issued citations to the chaperones for "destruction of wildlife." Later, the group's chaperones claimed that they themselves had been throwing stones at the bear to keep it away from the group's food, which had been improperly stored. They said one of the stones *accidentally* hit the bear in the head, killing it.

While no one in Yosemite is known to have been killed by a bear, more than a few people have been killed by horses. In addition to John Hutchings, who was killed when his team was spooked and threw him from his carriage, there have been several other people killed in Yosemite by horses. One of the first of these incidents occurred in 1867 when former gold rush prospector John Anderson was kicked in the head by a horse—some say it was a mule. Anderson, who had worked in Yosemite since the mid-1850s, died instantly.

During its early years, Yosemite National Park was patrolled and more or less operated by the U.S. Army. Most of the troopers posted to Yosemite were seasoned cavalrymen who knew as much about horses as anyone. Even so, horse-related accidents happened, and occasionally they resulted in serious injury. In one such incident, Private Chattem Rochette of the 4th U.S. Cavalry Regiment was thrown from his horse while patrolling the Yosemite backcountry. Rochette's fall did not kill him outright, but he had several broken bones and took a heavy blow to the head. Rochette died less than twenty-four hours later, most likely from a brain hemorrhage.

Horses have also killed Yosemite tourists. In 1916 twenty-three-year-old May Pewing died from a fall she took while riding a horse in Yosemite Valley. Likely she had a broken neck. In 1980 thirty-one-year old Karen Hardage was thrown by a spooked horse west of Tenaya. There were several other riders accompanying Hardage that day, and whatever had spooked her horse startled their mounts as well. One of them kicked Hardage in the head, killing her. As recently as 1992, a two-year-old boy named Garren Walbridge was killed in Yosemite Valley when he fell off a pony. The pony was being led by the boy's mother when something spooked the animal. It ran, dragging the child for a considerable distance. Little Garren died of head injuries.

People have even been killed by deer in Yosemite. Just such an incident took place in 1977 not far from the Wawona Hotel. While picnicking with his parents, five-year-old Colin Neu became fascinated by a mule deer that had been attracted by the smell of salty food. The boy was attempting to feed the deer a potato chip when something frightened the animal. The deer jerked its head up violently, skewering the boy with one of its antlers. The sharp antler penetrated the boy's chest and ruptured an artery. The boy died before medical help arrived.

FATAL PROTEST

1998

Early in the morning on June 9, 1998, Frank Gambalie III was taking in a view that few Yosemite visitors ever get to enjoy. Standing on the summit of El Capitan, he was able to gaze out over Yosemite Valley as it first became visible in the gathering dawn. However, Gambalie was not here to contemplate the scenery. He had something else in mind altogether. As soon as there was enough light for him to clearly see the ground spreading out before him more than 3,500 feet below, Gambalie stepped forward and jumped.

What Gambalie experienced during the next few moments has often been described by others who have tried it, but they all say it cannot be adequately put into words. He was in free fall. Speeding toward the earth, he seemed to be suspended in air. Then Gambalie pulled his rip cord, his parachute snapped open above his head, and he drifted more or less gently to the ground.

Once on his feet again, Gambalie quickly gathered his gear. He knew he had to hurry because he was only too well aware that he had just broken the law. There is a federal law against what is called "illegal air delivery," and breaking it is considered a misdemeanor. The applicable federal code reads as follows:

CODE OF FEDERAL REGULATIONS
TITLE 36 - PARKS, FORESTS, AND PUBLIC
PROPERTY
CHAPTER 1 - NATIONAL PARK SERVICE,
DEPARTMENT OF THE INTERIOR
PART 2 - RESOURCE PROTECTION, PUBLIC
USE AND RECREATION

36 CFR 2.17 - Aircraft and Air Delivery
(a) The following are prohibited:

. . . 3. Delivering or retrieving a person or object by parachute, helicopter, or other airborne means, except in emergencies involving public safety or serious property loss, or pursuant to the terms and conditions of a permit.

Gambalie had very much hoped to avoid dealing with any law enforcement authorities on this day. That's why he had made his jump so early. However, he was in for a shock. Yosemite park officials had been expecting someone to try a jump that morning, and two park rangers were lying in wait. Alerted by the sight of Gambalie's parachute, they emerged from their hiding place in the bushes and attempted to make an arrest. They did not succeed, and the tragic sequence of events that followed would cost the young jumper his life.

To avoid arrest, Gambalie ran off toward the Merced River with the rangers in hot pursuit. Caught between the rangers and the river's swirling waters, Gambalie jumped in and tried to swim across to the other side. He never made it. For some reason he could not stay afloat and very soon disappeared beneath the rushing river waters. Rescue attempts and searches for Gambalie's body proved unsuccessful. About a month later, his body would be found in the river only about 100 yards from the spot where he was last seen. Frank Gambalie's fate was highly ironic for he had survived a leap from a rock more than two-thirds of a mile high only to die in a bizarre drowning incident.

The sport that Gambalie was participating in that day is called BASE (an acronym for Buildings, Antennae, Spans, and Earth) jumping. Most parachutists jump from small airplanes, but BASE jumpers leap from buildings, bridges, cliffs, and similar tall, fixed objects. Because of the extreme danger involved in BASE jumping, it is illegal almost everywhere. Some years before Gambalie's jump, the sport was tested over a six-month period in Yosemite, after which it was banned as too dangerous. The law supporting the ban imposes a fine of up to $5,000 and six months in jail, plus the loss of the jumper's gear.

However, the sort of adventurers willing to face the risks involved in BASE jumping are unlikely to be discouraged by the threat of fines or even jail time. To pursue their sport while avoiding detection by the authorities, BASE jumpers climb mountains in the dark and jump just before dawn. BASE jumping is an extreme sport and involves great risk to the jumper, but those who have done it say the adrenaline rush they get from a jump keeps them coming back for more. At the time of Gambalie's drowning, there had been a reported twenty-one deaths of BASE jumpers in national parks around the country. His was the only death not directly related to the jump itself.

Following the Gambalie tragedy, a group of BASE jumpers planned a memorial jump off El Capitan to protest the young man's death. They wanted to make the point that other extreme sports such as rock climbing and hang gliding are also very dangerous but are not banned in most national parks. Hearing of the protest, park officials decided to let it go forward on the theory that it would be much safer if it were carried out in a structured manner and if authorities were present. An agreement between the park and the jumpers designated Friday, October 22, 1998, as the day for the event. Jumpers understood that they would be arrested and have their equipment confiscated as soon as they landed. A target landing area was selected and a ranger's hat placed within it. The hat would be autographed by each jumper once they'd safely reached the ground.

About 150 spectators were on hand, and they were in a celebratory mood. In fact, the jumps were being filmed by Tom Sanders, a stuntman and documentary filmmaker whose wife, Jan Davis, was to be the fourth of five jumpers. The rangers escorted the jumpers up El Capitan, and the first three made their jumps without incident. With each jump, the crowd cheered and saluted the jumpers with approving "high fives."

Then it was Jan Davis's turn. Like her husband, Davis worked in the film stunt industry. She had successfully completed several BASE jumps in the past and avoided capture. Her parachute and other jumping gear were excellent and expensive. Not wanting it to be confiscated, she borrowed some equipment from another jumper. This turned out to have been the first of two fatal mistakes. The second mistake was her decision not to wear a backup parachute, even though El Capitan was high enough to make its use possible in an emergency—in some cases BASE jumpers don't have time to make use of an emergency chute.

Using unfamiliar equipment and lacking a backup, Jan Davis leapt from the summit of El Capitan. Below, in a matter of just a few seconds, the crowd's cheers and merriment turned to grief. As her husband filmed the jump, Jan Davis's parachute failed to open, and since there was no backup chute, the result was inevitable. Davis died on impact with the talus slope at the bottom of El Capitan.

Instead of jumping, the last of the protesters decided to walk down the mountain. For their organized act of civil disobedience, each of the protesters was fined $2,000 and each had their chutes and other equipment confiscated. Additionally, they agreed to pay the $6,000 cost for removal of Jan Davis's body.

YOUNG CLIMBER SACRIFICES
HIMSELF FOR A FRIEND

1999

When Peter Tebush, Kerry Pyle, and Joseph Kerwin began their climb at Glacier Point on the morning of Sunday, June 13, 1999, they focused their attention on the sheer and deeply impressive cliff face. Foremost in their thoughts was a simple concern: how they would find their way up to the summit. Probably it never would have occurred to them that they would soon be ambushed by calamity—and death.

On vacation from their college in Gunnison, Colorado, Tebush, Pyle, and Kerwin were all experienced climbers. A few days earlier, the three young climbers had attempted an ascent of El Capitan but had been forced to turn back when a rope broke. There was not enough time left for another try at El Capitan, so rather than go home to Colorado disappointed, they decided to climb Glacier Point instead. The Glacier Point ascent was shorter and easier, but an adventure nonetheless. They figured it would provide a fine consolation for their failed effort to conquer El Capitan.

Like so many young adventurers who come to Yosemite, Tebush, Pyle, and Kerwin were sturdy, fun-loving, and perhaps just a touch reckless. At one point during their stay, they had strung a tightrope between two trees so they could hone their balancing skills. They even welcomed other campers to try it out, which many did. More than a few wobbled and fell, much to the amusement of all concerned.

Now, as they faced Glacier Point, their thoughts turned to more serious matters. They were well prepared for the climb, had all the proper gear, and knew how to use it. They figured they were quite capable of reaching the top, and this they did by following "The Apron Jam," a well-established climber route.

Having reached the summit and congratulated one another on the accomplishment, the three began their descent. They had almost completed it when they were forced to deal with the factor that plays a role in nearly every outdoor disaster—the unexpected. Neither they nor anyone in the park could have predicted that a portion of the cliff, created millions of years earlier by a glacier, would choose this time to give way. Kerwin and Terbush were already on the ground when the rocks began to fall, but Pyle was still dangling from a rope some 60 feet above the earth. As it happened, Terbush was tethering the rope that held Pyle and kept him from plunging to the surface below.

When the rockslide started, Kerwin saw it and ran for his life. He managed to get far enough from the wall of Glacier Point to avoid the deadly rocks. Terbush, on the other hand, faced a horrifying decision. If he released the rope and ran, Pyle would fall and very likely be killed. If he held onto the rope, Terbush himself would almost certainly be crushed. No one will ever know what went through Terbush's mind when he made his decision, but make it he did. Terbush held the rope and stood his ground.

A moment later Terbush all but disappeared beneath a pile of rocks and rubble that had fallen from the cliff face. Some of the rocks would later be described by a tearful Pyle as "Volkswagen-sized." They had crushed the life out of Pyle's brave friend. Pyle understood only too well that his friend had sacrificed his own life to save him.

Choked by the enormous cloud of dust thrown up by the slide, Kerwin and Pyle raced for help, but to no avail. In nearby Curry Village, the thunderous roar and crash of the boulders breaking away from the cliff had shocked and frightened family campers, many of whom were just settling down to dinner. Within moments the panicked campers, along with much of that part of the park, were engulfed in swirling dust. Soon after, amid the screams of frightened children, could be heard the shouts of a young man. It was Pyle. "My buddy's dead!" he cried.

Help eventually arrived, but of course, it was too late. According to the reports of would-be rescuers, Terbush still held the climbing rope tightly in his hands when his body was recovered.

The June 1999 rockslide brought some 279 cubic yards or about 660 tons of broken rock crashing down into the valley. By Yosemite standards, it was not a particularly large slide, and except for the death of Terbush, not unusually destructive.

Rockslides are an ever present danger in Yosemite. They have killed before and will likely do so again.

Rockslides are part of the process that created the mountains and the valley and now are tearing them down. The process began as much as twenty million years ago when molten rock crystallized into granite. Movement of the earth's crust then forced the rock to the surface, where glaciers eventually carved the magnificent cliffs we see today. Tremendous pressures inside the rocks sometimes cause them to give way and come crashing down. This is known as exfoliation. Normally a slow and methodical process, exfoliation of rock may be speeded up by water that runs into the crevices and cracks of the cliff. The water often freezes at night, causing layers of rock to peel away. Perhaps not coincidentally, the spring of 1999 had been exceptionally damp and cold. Earthquakes may also speed up the process of exfoliation. There had been two small tremors during the months before the June 1999 slide.

The fact is, however, the rock fall that took the life of young Terbush, was part of a whole series of falls at Glacier Point that had begun almost a year earlier. On November 16, 1998, 736 cubic yards or 1,738 tons of rock fell more than 1,000 feet at Glacier Point and came within a few yards of crushing tents and campers in Camp Curry. Then, beginning in May the following year and extending well into July, there were several more falls. One of these ended in tragedy for three young Colorado climbers.

FATAL ATTEMPT TO
FLY LIKE A BIRD

2001

Although it was late summer, the early morning air was chilly up near the base of Half Dome where four Spanish rock climbers huddled around their campfire. Bracing themselves for the day's climb with mugs of steaming coffee, they were enjoying the warmth of the first rays of the morning sun, which was just then rising over peaks in the east. Just as they were about to shoulder their gear for their assault on the cliffs, one of the climbers pointed out an interesting sight to his friends. Someone appeared to be standing on the precipice of Half Dome far overhead. His arms were spread, as if he intended to flap them and fly like a bird out over Yosemite Valley.

Then, in full view of all four climbers, whose mouths were by this time ajar, an incredible thing happened. The man jumped from the cliff and dove straight down, his body swept back in a position much like that of a high diver. The fall lasted only a few seconds, but to the climbers watching it seemed to last much longer. For them, the fall seemed to last forever, like the climax of an emotionally painful movie, one they wished they had never seen at all. Finally, this extraordinary drama came to a sudden and stomach-wrenching end little more than 200 feet from the climbers' camp as the diver struck the rocks with a sickening thud.

It was 6:30 a.m. on August 17, 2001, and Vladimir Boutkovski had accomplished his purpose. He had just freed his spirit from its earthly, physical bonds. He had also, unintentionally, caused four Spanish climbers to abandon any thought of further mountaineering on that day. They quickly struck camp and descended to Yosemite Valley where they reported the incident. By 9:30 a.m. a helicopter with a search and rescue team was headed for Half Dome.

At the base of the great granite monument the team found the jumper's crushed body. However, little of what they found either on the corpse or nearby answered the questions that wracked their brains. Who was this young man and why had he done this horrifying thing?

It took several days to answer the first question. A fingerprint match identified the jumper as Vladimir Boutkovski, a twenty-four-year-old employee of a Silicon Valley computer company. A recent Russian immigrant, Boutkovski had lived with his family in Santa Clara. He was not married.

The second question might never be answered. What had caused Boutkovski to jump or fall from the 4,000-foot-high rock formation? At first, investigators regarded the tragic incident as a failed BASE jumping attempt, but since no parachute or other BASE jumping equipment was located, suicide seemed a more likely explanation. As more information about Boutkovski emerged, however, the young man's end came to be viewed as something very different from a typical suicide.

Apparently, Boutkovski had not been depressed or in ill health. His employment was secure, he did not owe large sums of money, and there was no evidence of emotional stress such as that caused, for instance, by a broken engagement or a ruined love affair. By all accounts, Boutkovski had been a relatively happy young man. So why would he take his own life?

The answer may lie in the works and philosophy of author Carlos Castaneda, whose best-selling book *The Teachings of Don Juan* inspired a generation of young mystics. Boutkovski and some of his closest friends were big fans of Castaneda and took his books very seriously indeed. They believed that by following the mystic path described by Castaneda's Don Juan, they could free their *inner spirits* and live a better life. Many critics consider Castaneda's books to be entertaining novels rather than serious works of philosophy, but Boutkovski and his friends certainly thought of them as the real thing.

On more than one occasion prior to August 2001, Boutkovski told acquaintances that he might attempt to free his spirit by jumping from some high place. Perhaps the young man thought he truly could fly like a bird if only he had the courage to make the attempt. Or maybe he felt the spiritual realm would embrace him as he plunged headlong to earth. We'll never know whether it did or not, but one thing is clear: Boutkovski's body did not long survive the experience.

On the day before the incident, Boutkovski expropriated a friend's automobile and drove off toward Yosemite. He left behind a note that hinted vaguely at his intentions. "I'm going to undertake an endeavor of possibly utmost stupidity," he said. "Let me just say that if this is the only thing you see from me, then look for your car at the Yosemite Park near the shop. The key will be in the exhaust pipe."

That is the last anyone heard of Vladimir Boutkovski. His friend's car was found exactly where he had said it would be, with the keys in the exhaust pipe. Apparently, Boutkovski had taken his own life, but was it a suicide? Probably that depends on your point of view.

Of course, Boutkovski was neither the first nor the last to intentionally kill himself in Yosemite National Park. Dozens, if not hundreds, of people have chosen to end their existence in the dramatic and beautiful surroundings offered by Yosemite Valley and the cliffs that enclose it. Some Yosemite suicides, such as forty-two-year-old Bruce Cook who died in Yosemite Village on Christmas Day in 1910, have chosen to shoot themselves. But suicide is by nature a matter of personal choice, and the methods of ending one's own life are as varied as the people who make this grim decision. For instance, Peter Arioli, who died in March 1919, blew himself up with several sticks of dynamite. Berkeley chemistry student Vincent Herkomer, who killed himself at the base of Half Dome in 1930, appropriately enough swallowed poison. In 1963 Arthur Ellson, aged fifty-nine, hung himself from an overhead beam in his cabin. In 1977 thirty-six-year-old Mohammed Faeghi camped out near the Happy Isles Nature Center, got drunk on vodka, crawled into his sleeping bag, and cut his own throat.

Vladimir Boutkovski was also not the first to intentionally jump from a Yosemite cliff. James Stergar, age thirty, jumped off Half Dome on August 25, 1956, leaving a suicide note in his car. In 1973 a depressed twenty-year-old named Linden Moore is believed to have jumped from Glacier Point. In 1985 a distraught thirty-year-old named Richard Mughir first murdered his wife and then ended his own life by jumping off Glacier Point. There have been many such tragedies in Yosemite National Park. Those listed here represent only a small percentage of them.

DARING BLIZZARD
RESCUES

2004

Weather is a matter of interest to practically everyone on the planet, but in Yosemite it is a special concern. The weather in Yosemite can change dramatically from one day, one hour, or even one minute to the next, and if the wrong sort of weather catches an unprepared hiker out in the wilderness or a climber out on an exposed ledge, the results can be deadly. National park rangers know this, and they warn park visitors to take likely changes in the weather into account when planning their activities. When warnings aren't enough and people's lives are threatened by a sudden onslaught of bad weather, then rangers must go to the rescue.

On October 19, 2004, Keith Lober, head of search and rescue at Yosemite National Park, studied the rock face of El Capitan, looking for climbers trapped by a severe autumn snow storm that had blown unexpectedly in the Sierra. As if out of nowhere, the storm had swept over the park early on October 17 and then held Yosemite in its icy grip for several days. The blizzard had now been blowing for two solid days, and a number of visitors were either known to be stranded or missing.

Using a powerful scope, Lober found what he was looking for—two climbers approximately 2,000 feet up the cliff face. He had been keeping a careful watch on them. He wasn't sure how much experience they had with conditions like these, and he wasn't sure how much equipment they had with them. Had they been prepared for a blizzard? Probably not, and what Lober saw when he trained his scope on the climbers now was deeply troubling. They were not moving.

For two days, he had watched the two climbers, hanging from the cliff, waiting out the storm. There was nothing that he could do at this point but monitor their whereabouts, because any rescue attempt would have to wait for better weather. There was so much snow and wind that a helicopter could not safely fly into the area to see what was happening.

Then, suddenly, he saw the two start climbing again. "It told me they were desperate," said Lober. He understood that unless they were in terrible trouble, the climbers would have stayed where they were until the weather improved. At least, that is what they would have done if they were still thinking clearly. Realizing their situation might now be critical, Lober launched a rescue operation immediately.

By this time, the blinding snow had turned into torrential rain. Teams began to hike up toward the summit, a treacherous climb in itself due to both the snowfall and the rain that would surely freeze when temperatures plunged again that evening. For hour after hour the teams struggled on, knowing that lives likely depended on their reaching their destination while there was still time to take effective action.

Meanwhile, Lober had grown concerned about another climber, Dave Turner, an all-year mountaineer who was stuck on a ledge just above the Nose, a 40-foot outcropping 100 feet below the summit.

But Turner, who had been up there on the side of El Capitan for seventeen days, was a regular, and he had worn proper clothes for the weather. What is more, Turner had kept in touch by radio. He had refused help up to now, but with the change to rain, he, too, had decided it was time to call for help.

The rescuers climbed 11 miles that Tuesday to the summit and then waited there for the weather to clear enough to rappel down to Turner, who by this time was drenched. Having been unable to contact the Japanese tourists whom he had passed on his climb, Turner realized that he, too, might now be in danger. First, the rescuers pulled Turner to safety on the summit, where he received hot liquids, food, and medical attention and spent the night. The following day he was brought down by helicopter.

Next the helicopter attempted to rescue the Japanese climbers, but it was too late. The two were found dangling from their ropes clasped in a frozen embrace. "The man had his arms around his partner as though he had been trying to warm her," says park ranger Scott Gediman. "When you think what they went through with the cold and the rain and the snow, it makes it even more heartbreaking."

A rescuer climbed down to retrieve the couple's bodies. Short and thin, they fit together into one yellow carrier that was hauled to the top for the long, quiet hike down. Afterwards there was much speculation concerning their deaths, for the couple's digital camera told an unusual story. Twenty-six-year-old Ryoichi Yamamoto, an experienced mountaineer according to witnesses to his climb, and Moriko Ryugo, a novice, had been relatively secure at Camp Six, just below the famous Nose that sticks out below the Summit. Their equipment and sleeping bags were dry and their food supplies plentiful. They seemed to have been relatively safe and comfortable.

What had happened? Why had they suddenly exposed themselves to the extreme danger of a climb in such horrible weather conditions?

Perhaps the novice started to feel hemmed in by her location. Although dry and cozy, someone unused to such a confined space might find it too difficult to bear. We will never know for certain, but their decision to start climbing again proved a fatal one.

When the rescuers found the couple, they were tied to a knob of granite only a short distance above Camp Six. They could have easily rappelled back to the camp, but instead they were dangling from this knob, exposed to the elements. Their equipment bag was gone. What had happened?

The answer may lie in the couple's mental state. People suffering from hypothermia often make poor choices, and the colder they get, the less likely they are to make reasonable decisions. Numbness and unconsciousness can come quickly in the conditions the climbers faced during those last fateful and fatal days. We will never know exactly how their lives ended—or why.

BIBLIOGRAPHY

Books

Beatty, Matthew Edward. *Bears of Yosemite.* Yosemite: Yosemite Natural History Association, 1943.

Bingaman, John. *The Ahwahneechees: A Story of the Yosemite Indians.* Lodi, California: End-Kian Publishing Company, 1961.

Brower, Kenneth. *Yosemite: An American Treasure.* Washington, DC: National Geographic Society, 1997.

Bunnell, Lafayette Houghton. *Discovery of the Yosemite and the Indian War of 1851 Which Led to That Event.* Reprint of 1880 edition. Freeport, New York: Books for Libraries Press, 1971 edition.

Burgess, Jack A. *Trains to Yosemite.* Berkeley and Wilton, California: Signature Press, 2005.

Chamberlain, Newell D. *The Call of Gold: True Tales on the Gold Road to Yosemite.* Mariposa, California: Gazette Press, 1936.

Demars, Stanford E. *The Tourist in Yosemite 1855–1985.* Salt Lake City: University of Utah Press, 1991.

Denny, Glen. *Yosemite in the Sixties.* Santa Barbara, California: T. Adler Books/Patagonia, Inc., 2007.

Duane, Daniel. *El Capitan—Historic Feats and Radical Routes.* San Francisco: Chronicle Books, 2000.

Ghiglieri, Michael Patrick. *Off the Wall: Death in Yosemite: Gripping Accounts of All Known Fatal Mishaps in America's First Protected Land of Scenic Wonders.* Flagstaff, Arizona: Puma Press, LLC, 2007.

Goldstein, Milton. *The Magnificent West: Yosemite.* New York: Arch Cape Press, 1988.

Goodwin, Mark. *Yosemite: The 100-Year Flood.* Mariposa, California: Sierra Press, 1997.

Gyer, Jack. *Yosemite, Saga of a Century: 1864–1964.* Oakhurst, California: Sierra Star Press, 1964.

Hubbard, Douglass. *Ghost Mines of Yosemite.* Fredericksburg, Texas: The Awani Press, 1958.

Huber, Norman King. *The Geologic Story of Yosemite National Park.* Washington: Government Printing Office, 1987.

Johnston, Hank and James Law. *Railroads of the Yosemite Valley, sixth edition.* Yosemite National Park: Yosemite Assn/Heyday Books, 1998.

Jones, William R. *Yosemite.* Las Vegas: KC Publications, 1971.

Madgic, Bob and Adrian Estaban. *Shattered Air: A True Account of Catastrophe and Courage on Yosemite's Half Dome.* Short Hills, New Jersey: Burford Books, 2007.

Meyerson, Harvey. *Nature's Army: When Soldiers Fought for Yosemite.* Lawrence: University Press of Kansas, 2001.

Misuraca, Karen. *Insiders' Guide to Yosemite,* third edition. Guilford, Connecticut: Globe Pequot Press, 2006.

Muir, John. *The Yosemite.* San Francisco: Sierra Club Books, 1988.

Neider, Susan M. *Wild Yosemite.* New York: Skyhorse Publishing, 2007.

Olmsted, Frederick Law. *Yosemite and the Mariposa Grove: A Preliminary Report, 1865.* Yosemite: Yosemite Association, 1995.

Paden, Irene Dakin and Schlichtmann, Margaret Elizabeth. *The Big Oak Flat Road: An Account of Freighting from Stockton to Yosemite Valley.* Oakland, California: Schlichtmann, 1955.

Roper, Steve. *Camp 4: Recollections of a Yosemite Rockclimber.* Seattle: Mountaineers Books, 1998.

Rose, Gene. *Yosemite's Tioga Country: A History and Appreciation.* Yosemite National Park: Yosemite Association/Heyday Books, 2006.

Runte, Alfred. *Yosemite: The Embattled Wilderness.* Lincoln: University of Nebraska Press, 1990.

Russell, Carl P. *One Hundred Years in Yosemite. Omnibus edition.* Yosemite National Park: Yosemite Association, 1992.

Sanborn, Margaret. *Yosemite: Its Discovery, Its Wonders and Its People.* New York: Random House, 1981.

Sargent, Shirley. *The Ahwahnee Hotel.* Yosemite: Yosemite Park and Curry Co., 1990.

Schaffer, Jeffrey P. *Yosemite: The Valley and Surrounding Uplands, seventh edition.* Berkeley, California: Wilderness Press, 2006.

Simpson, John W. *Dam! Water, Power, Politics, and Preservation in Hetch Hetchy and Yosemite National Park.* New York: Pantheon Books, 2005.

Starr, Kevin. *California, A History.* New York: The Modern Library, 2005.

Taylor, Katherine Ames. *Yosemite Tales and Trails.* Sacramento, California: H. S. Crocker Co., Inc., 1934.

Trexler, Keith A. *The Tioga Road: A History 1883–1961.* Yosemite National Park: Yosemite Natural History Association. 1961, 1980.

United States National Park Service. *Yosemite National Park, California, Official Map and Guide.* Washington, DC: The Service, 1997.

Walklet, Keith. *The Ahwahnee: Yosemite's Grand Hotel.* Yosemite National Park, California: DNC Parks & Resorts at Yosemite and Yosemite Association, 2004.

Wilkins, Thurman. *John Muir: Apostle of Nature.* Norman, Oklahoma: University of Oklahoma Press, 1995.

Wuerthner, George. *Yosemite: The Grace and Grandeur.* Stillwater, Minnesota: Voyageur Press, 2002.

Zwinger, Ann. *Yosemite: Valley of Thunder.* San Diego, California: Thunder Bay Press, 1996.

Periodicals and Web sites

Baer, Warren. "A Trip to Yosemite Falls." *Mariposa Democrat,* August 5, 1856.

"Camp 4 Listed with National Register of Historic Places." Yosemite National Park News Release, February 27, 2003.

Cohen, Michael. "Stormy Sermons." *The Pacific Historian,* Volume 25 Issue 2 (1981): 21–36.

Binkley, Clark S. "Forestry in a Postmodern World or Just What Was John Muir Doing Running a Sawmill in Yosemite Valley?" *Policy Sciences,* Vol. 31, No. 2 (1998): 133–144.

Boyer, David. "Yosemite—Forever?" *National Geographic,* Volume 117, No. 1 (January 1985): 52–79.

Brockman, C. Frank. "Park Naturalists and the Evolution of National Park Service Interpretation through World War II." *Journal of Forest History,* Vol. 22, No. 1 (January 1978): 24–43.

"California National Parks Centennial: Special Issue." *California History,* No. 69 (Summer 1990).

Clements, Kendrick A. "Politics and the Park: San Francisco's Fight for Hetch Hetchy, 1908–1913." *The Pacific Historical Review,* Vol. 48, No. 2 (May 1979): 185–215.

"Flood of 1997 and Flood Recovery." Yosemite Association Web site: www.yosemite.org/79/Flood-of-1997.htm?expandable=3.

Fragnoli, Delaine. "Naming Yosemite." *ATQ.* Vol. 18, No. 4 (December 2004): 263–275.

Goodrum, Janet. "The Miwoks of California." *The Pacific Historian.* Vol. 13, Issue 4 (1969): 38–46.

Grusin, Richard A. "Recreating Yosemite." *Culture, Technology, and the Creation of America's National Parks.* Cambridge, UK: Cambridge University Press, 2004.

Hampton, H. Duane. "Opposition to National Parks." *Journal of Forest History,* Vol. 25, No. 1 (January 1981): 36–45.

———. "The Army and the National Parks." *Montana: The Magazine of Western History,* Vol. 22, No. 3, Yellowstone: The First Century (Summer 1972): 64–79.

Heat-Moon, William Least and Phil Schermeister. "Beyond the Valley of Wonders." *National Geographic,* Vol. 207, Issue 1 (January 2005): 98–117.

Hendricks, Gordon. "Bierstadt's The Domes of the Yosemite." *American Art Journal,* Vol. 3, No. 2 (Autumn 1971): 23–31.

"Hetch Hetchy: Time to Redeem a Historic Mistake." Sierra Club Web site: www.sierraclub.org/ca/hetchhetchy/.

Huntley-Smith, Jen. "Water in Print: Nature and Artifice." *Agricultural History,* Vol. 76, No. 2, Water and Rural History (Spring 2002): 354–363.

Huth, Hans. "The American and Nature." *Journal of the Warburg and Courtauld Institutes,* Vol. 13, No. 1/2 (1950): 101–149.

J. H. B. "Constitutional Law: Jurisdiction over Yosemite National Park." *California Law Review,* Vol. 27, No. 2 (January 1939): 208–211.

Johnson, D. W. "Hanging Valleys of the Yosemite. Part I." *Bulletin of the American Geographical Society,* Vol. 43, No. 11 (1911): 826–837.

———. "Hanging Valleys of the Yosemite. Part II." *Bulletin of the American Geographical Society,* Vol. 43, No. 12 (1911): 890–903.

Klyza, Christopher McGrory. "The United States Army, Natural Resources, and Political Development in the Nineteenth Century." *Polity,* Vol. 35, No. 1 (Autumn 2002): 1–28.

Moore, Barrington. "The Proposed Roosevelt-Sequoia National Park and the Barbour Bill." *Science,* New Series, Vol. 57, No. 1464 (Jan. 19, 1923): 82–84.

Nash, Roderick. "American Wilderness in Historical Perspective." *Forest History,* Vol. 6, No. 4 (Winter 1963): 2–13.

O'Brien, Bart. "Earthquakes or Snowflowers." *The Pacific Historian,* Vol. 29, Issue 2 (1985): 30–41.

Peterson, F. Ross. "Reviewed Work: Big Thompson: Profile of a Natural Disaster by David McComb." *The Western Historical Quarterly,* Vol. 13, No. 1 (January 1982): 79–80.

Spence, Mark. "Dispossessing the Wilderness: Yosemite Indians and the National Park Ideal. 1864–1930." *The Pacific Historical Review,* Vol. 65, No. 1 (February 1996): 27–59.

"Surveying Yosemite Valley: 'A Classic of Science.'" *The Science News Letter,* Vol. 20, No. 536 (July 18, 1931): 42–43.

Teisch, Jessica. "The Drowning of Big Meadows: Nature's Managers in Progressive-Era California." *Environmental History,* Vol. 4, No. 1 (January 1999): 32–53.

U.S. Department of the Interior. "Interior Department Estimates Cost to Repair Flood Damage at Yosemite National Park at $178 Million." *Science Blog,* January 31, 1997.

"Yosemite National Park Receives High Marks for Flood Recovery Efforts." Yosemite National Park News Release, March 30, 1999.

Newspapers

"2 Climbers Die on El Capitan—Rescuers Say Pair Had Inadequate Gear; Teams Check on Seven Others." *Modesto Bee* 21 October 2004.

"4-Bidding Heights—Historic Campground at Yosemite Spawned Rock-Climbing Revolution." *Daily News of Los Angeles* 22 May 2003. Valley rop ed.: S12. Retrieved February 27, 2009.

"10 Years After Fires, Yosemite Showing Its Resilience." *Modesto Bee* 11 September 2000, All, B: B1. Retrieved February 1, 2009.

"A Battle over Park Water—Yosemite Is Seen Threatened by Dam." *San Jose Mercury News* 16 April 1986. Morning Final edition: 1. Retrieved February 27, 2009.

"A Boulder Move— Climbers Are Forgoing Bigger Rocks and Turning Attention to Bouldering." *Fresno Bee* 17 May 2006. Final edition: D8. Retrieved February 27, 2009.

"Alternate for Hetch Hetchy Water / Sierra Club Proposes Tapping Downstream Tuolumne Reservoir." *San Jose Mercury News* 9 August 1987. Morning Final ed.: 12B.

"'Another Way to Ski' and Then Some." *Fresno Bee* 24 February 1989, Home, Lifestyle: E1.

"At Camp 4-$H_2$0: Go with the Flow." *Merced Sun-Star* 1 August 2005: 01. Retrieved February 27, 2009.

"Autumn Color Close to Home." *Modesto Bee* 24 October 1997. All editions: G-1. Retrieved February 27, 2009.

"Bill to Slow Yosemite Damming Gains." *Sacramento Bee* 11 September 1986. Metro Final edition: A7. Retrieved February 27, 2009.

"Bill Would Bar Hetch Hetchy Water System Growth." *Sacramento Bee* 4 March 1987. Metro Final edition: B10. Retrieved February 27, 2009.

Bishop, Katherine. "Closing of Yosemite Renews Debate over Fire Policies." *New York Times* 16 August 1990, Late edition (East Coast).

Bizjak, Tony. "No Escape from Civilization—Crowded Yosemite Lures Campers Who Like to Be Pampered." *San Francisco Chronicle* 12 August 1987. Final edition: 19. Retrieved February 27, 2009.

"Climber Died Saving a Friend—Yosemite Slide Turns Outing into Tragedy." *Sacramento Bee* 15 June 1999. Metro Final edition: A1. Retrieved February 27, 2009.

"Climbers Agitate to Save Sport's Yosemite Mecca." *Contra Costa Times* 13 September 1999. Final edition: A08. Retrieved February 27, 2009.

"Climbers Exchanging Help for Free Camping—Yosemite: They Get to Stay for Free but Are on Call to Help Rescue People in Trouble." *Ventura County Star* 31 July 1998. Ventura edition: A04. Retrieved February 27, 2009.

"Climbers Sue Yosemite over New Buildings, They Say They Just Want to Preserve the Tranquility of a Campground and Nearby Climbing Sites." *Fresno Bee* 29 May 1998.

"Conquest of Capitan—Climbing Enthusiasts Will Gather to Remember the Moments That Led Up to Taming of a Landmark." *Fresno Bee* 6 November 2008. South Valley edition: D8.

"Construction Will Bring About Change to Park." *Merced Sun-Star* 23 February 2004.

"Deadly Floods Threaten More Damage in Valley * One Valley Woman Dies." *Fresno Bee* 4 January 1997. Home edition: A1.

della Cava, Marco R. "The Flooding of Yosemite." *USA Today,* June 7, 2002.

Dicker, Ron. "Getting Life on High / Daredevils Fall for Adventure in Big Way—Off Skyscrapers, Cliffs, Bridges." *Orange County Register* 23 October 1986 Evening Edition.

"'Easy' Is Subjective When Traversing El Capitan." *Contra Costa Times* 1 May 2005. Final edition: E01.

"Expert Fears More Slides at Yosemite." *Modesto Bee* 17 June 1999. All edition: 1. Retrieved February 27, 2009.

Ferrin, Lynn. "The Lion in Winter / Yosemite Valley Reflects a Serene Power in the Off-Season." *San Diego Union-Tribune* 13 January 2002. 1,2,3 edition: D-1.

Fimrite, Peter. "History Made 50 Years Ago Atop El Capitan." *San Francisco Chronicle* 9 November 2008. 5star edition: B1.

———. "Up for a Climbing Record." *San Francisco Chronicle* 26 June 2008. 5star-2dot edition: A1. Retrieved February 27, 2009.

———. "Yosemite Search and Rescue Pioneer Honored by U.S. for Decades of Heroism." *San Francisco Chronicle* 30 October 2008. 5star-dot edition: A1.

———. "Yosemite's New Breed of 'Rock Rats'." *San Francisco Chronicle* 10 September 2006. Final edition: A1.

"Finally, Climbers Finish Ascent * The Climb That Held the Nation's Attention Comes to an End After 13 Grueling Days." *Fresno Bee* 17 September 1991, Home, Telegraph: A1.

"Flashbacks from Here and There: Hit and Misses: The Arches." *Chico Enterprise-Record* 17 December 2001.

Fredman, Herb. "Debunking Fables about State Water." (San Diego) *Evening Tribune* 26 March 1986. 1,2,3,4,5,6 edition: B-9.

"Free-solo Rock Climbers Feel Spiritual Lure Toward a Hobby That Puts Them on the Edge of Oblivion." *Fresno Bee* 8 April 2004. Final edition: D1.

Gilliam, Harold. "John Muir, Compromiser." *San Francisco Chronicle* 13 January 1985. Sunday edition: 17.

"Gold! 150 Years Later and the Fever Still Burns." *Fresno Bee* 25 January 1998. Home edition: A1. Retrieved February 27, 2009.

"Graffiti Cracks Hetch Hetchy Dam." *San Francisco Chronicle* 21 July 1987. Final edition: 5. Retrieved February 27, 2009.

"Granite Slabs Poised to Fall at Yosemite." *Contra Costa Times* 22 June 1999. Final edition: A06.

"Grip on Yosemite—Activists Opposing Park Service Plans Cause Long Delays, Create Own Successes." *Modesto Bee* 2 February 2007. All editions: B1.

"Growing Threat of New Yosemite Slide." *Sacramento Bee* 22 June 1999. Metro Final edition: B1.

"Guarding the National Park." *New York Times* 17 October 1892.

"Half Dome Climbers 75 Feet Away * Paraplegic Park Ranger and His Partner Expect to Finish the Ascent This Morning." *Fresno Bee* 16 September 1991, Home, Metro: B1.

Hall, Carl T. "Yosemite Death Plunge / Parachute Fails During Stunt Protesting Ban on Jumps." *San Francisco Chronicle* 23 October 1999 Final Edition.

"Hodel Considers Plan to Drain Hetch Hetchy, Restore Valley." *San Jose Mercury News* 6 August 1987. Morning Final edition: 1A.

Keeler, Guy. "Trail to Awe: Yosemite's Tioga Road Has Been a Path to Nature's Preservation." *Fresno Bee* 22 February 2007.

"Lawmakers Nudge Yosemite to Rebuild." (Long Beach) *Press-Telegram* 17 November 2001. AM edition: A16.

Marshall, Roger. "Into the Jaws of Death." *San Francisco Chronicle* 2 June 1985. Sunday edition: 7. Retrieved February 27, 2009.

"Mountaineers Suing Yosemite." *Contra Costa Times* 30 May 1998. Final edition: A10. Retrieved February 27, 2009.

"Nightmare on Half Dome, Hikers Ignored Thunderclouds, Warning Signs." *San Jose Mercury News* 30 July 1985, Morning Final, Front: 1A.

Nolte, Carl. "$6 Billion Price Tag to Replace Hetch Hetchy." *San Francisco Chronicle* 7 August 1987. Final edition: 1. Retrieved February 27, 2009.

———. "The Rivers Ran Through It: The New Year's Storms—and the Floods That Came with Them—Washed a Lot of Misery into the Lives of the People Living Along the Central Valley's Highway 99, Where More Than One Tear Has Mixed with the Receding Brown Water." *San Francisco Chronicle* 26 January 1997. Sunday edition: 1/Z1. Retrieved February 27, 2009.

———. "Sierra Club's Alternative on Hetch Hetchy." *San Francisco Chronicle* 8 August 1987. Final edition: 1. Retrieved February 27, 2009.

——— and Susan Sward. "John Muir's Lost Valley—Before It Was Flooded." *San Francisco Chronicle* 7 August 1987. Final edition: 23.

"One Dead, 4 Injured in Yosemite Rockslide—1,400 Evacuated from Curry Village." *San Francisco Chronicle* 14 June 1999. Final edition: A1.

"Panel OKs Bill on Water Projects in Yosemite." *Fresno Bee* 11 September 1986. Home edition: D8.

"Parachutist Dies in Fall at Yosemite's El Capitan; Tragedy: A Santa Barbara Woman, 60, Leaps from the Cliff in Protest of a National Park Service Ban on Such Jumps. Chute Fails to Open as Husband Watches." *Los Angeles Times* 23 October 1999, Home edition.

"Paraplegic Climber Begins Challenge of El Capitan." *Fresno Bee* 20 July 1989, Home, Metro: A1.

"Paraplegic Climber May Reach Summit Today." *Fresno Bee* 26 July 1989, All, Metro: B1.

"Paraplegic Skiers Aim for Record—Cross-Country Athletes Traversing Yosemite." *Daily News of Los Angeles* 11 April 1993, Final, News: N3.

"Paraplegic's Climb Begins, Ranger and Friend Start up Half Dome * Park Ranger Who Pulled Himself up El Capitan Two Years Ago Is off on a Seven-Day Assault on Yosemite Symbol." *Fresno Bee* 5 September 1991, Home, Telegraph: A1.

"Park's Neighbor Protests Car Ban—Tuolumne Reacts to Yosemite Plan." *Modesto Bee,* 23 February 1998. All editions: 1.

"Park's Problems Are Urban in Nature * The Park Will Host 3.75 Million Visitors This Year, Leading to a City-Sized Burden." *Fresno Bee* 4 October 1992, Home, Telegraph: A1.

"Preserving Yosemite with Chisel and Law." *Bakersfield Californian* 16 November 2003: A1. Retrieved February 27, 2009.

"Probes of Park Slide Begin—Facility Not Subject to Outside Inspections, Experts Say." *Sacramento Bee* 4 June 1997. Metro Final edition: A1.

"Projects on Park's Horizon—Yosemite Will Reroute Traffic and Add Campsites." *Modesto Bee* 19 February 2004. All editions: B1.

"Rock Climbers Sue over New Yosemite Project—Lodging Would Be Built on Historic Campsite." *San Francisco Chronicle* 28 May 1998. Final editions: A19.

"Rockslide Threat Has Yosemite Valley on High Alert—Cracks Forming in Glacier Point's Tons of Granite Allow Geologists to Predict the Next Slide." *Fresno Bee* 30 June 1999. Home edition: A1.

Russell, Sabin. "Parachutist's Death Leaves Her Peers with Grief, Anger / Jumpers Debate Yosemite Tragedy." *San Francisco Chronicle* 25 October 1999 Final / East Bay Edition.

Sauer, Mark. "Paradise Lost? Power Vies with Glory in Yosemite Twin Valleys." *San Diego Union* 12 August 1987. 1,2,3,4,5,6 edition: E-1. Retrieved February 27, 2009.

"Seven Winter Things You Have to Do in Yosemite." (Pleasanton) *Tri-Valley Herald* 9 December 2007.

"S.F. Loses a Round in Hetch Hetchy Fight." *San Jose Mercury News* 15 August 1986. Morning Final edition: 1G.

"S.F.'s Hetch Hetchy Expansion Vetoed." *Sacramento Bee* 1 November 1984. Final edition: A04.

"S.F.'s Hetch Hetchy Water District Debates Cloud-Seeding in Dry Tuolumne Watershed." *San Jose Mercury News* 12 February 1987. Stock Final edition: 5C.

"Showing a Will of Granite Paraplegic, Partner Prove No Wall Is Too High to Scale." *Fresno Bee* 27 July 1989, Home, Metro: A1.

"Special Report—Yosemite—'People Love This Park.'" *Orange County Register* 6 April 1997. Morning edition: D08.

"Suit Targets Climber Haven—Group Wants Yosemite to Dump Building Plans." *Daily News of Los Angeles* 31 May 1998. Valley rop edition: N8.

"Summer Bus Plan Shelved for Yosemite Park." *San Francisco Chronicle* 6 October 1998. Final edition: A18.

"Taking Capitan: It's Been 50 Years." *Modesto Bee* 7 November 2008. All editions: A1.

Tawa, Renee. "The Three-Second Rush: Though Often Illegal, BASE jumping—Parachuting from Fixed Objects—Is Gaining Popularity." *Los Angeles Times* 24 March 2002, Home Edition.

"The Bold and the Boulders—Many Climbers Are Skipping Yosemite's Granite Walls and Scrambling up Smaller Formations Without Ropes." *Sacramento Bee* 1 June 2006. Metro Final edition: E1.

"The Nature vs. Tourism Debate No Longer Impedes a Massive Renovation Project in Yosemite Valley—Construction Ahead." *Fresno Bee* 21 September 2003. Final edition: A1.

"Trail Mix." *Fresno Bee* 4 September 2008. Final edition: D6. Retrieved February 27, 2009.

"U.S. Acts to Stop Any Expansion of Hetch Hetchy, Interior Department Rejects Power System Development." *San Jose Mercury News* 16 November 1985. Morning Final edition: 8B.

"Why Hetch Hetchy Valley Would Quickly Spring to Life." *San Jose Mercury News* 14 August 1987 Morning Final edition: 1A. Retrieved February 27, 2009.

"Wilson Forms Task Force on State's Flooding Woes." *Contra Costa Times* 7 June 1997. Final edition: A11. Retrieved February 27, 2009.

"Year-End Special: The Top Stories of 1997." *Contra Costa Times* 28 December 1997. Final edition: A25.

"Yosemite Autumn: A Year of Recovering from Disaster." (Santa Rosa) *Press Democrat* 16 October 1997. Final edition: D1. Retrieved February 27, 2009.

"Yosemite Campground Gets National Recognition." (Ontario) *Inland Valley Daily Bulletin* 27 February 2003.

"Yosemite Campgrounds Still a Bargain—Fee Increase for Camping Goes into Effect Next Month." *Modesto Bee* 6 January 2001. All editions: B1.

"Yosemite Climbers Camp Earns Historic Designation—Camp 4 Is Recognized as Starting Point of Many Famous Climbs." *Modesto Bee* 3 March 2003. All editions: B2.

"Yosemite Gets a Push to Rebuild." *Sacramento Bee* 19 November 2001. Metro Final edition: A3.

"Yosemite Lightning Kills 2, 3 Also Injured in 8 1/2-Mile Trek up Half Dome." *San Jose Mercury News* 29 July 1985, Morning Final, Front: 1A.

"Yosemite Makes Rock Solid Friendship—4 Decades After First Meeting, Tom Frost and Royal Robbins Still Enjoy Challenge of Climbing." *Modesto Bee* 16 April 2002. All editions: C1.

"Yosemite Proposal Loses Luster; Hodel's Idea Greeted with Skepticism." *Fresno Bee* 7 August 1987. Home edition: B1.

"Yosemite Rock Slide Found to Be Larger up to 162,000 Tons of Granite Broke Free." *San Jose Mercury News* 1 August 1996, Morning Final, California News: 3B.

"Yosemite Site Called Historic—Outdoors: Park's Camp 4 Lauded as Instrumental to Rock Climbing Development." *Long Beach Press-Telegram* 28 February 2003. AM edition: A11.

BIBLIOGRAPHY

"Yosemite Slide Took a Million Years to Form." *Contra Costa Times* 12 July 1996, Final, News: A01.

"Yosemite Under Siege—Rock Slides, Crime, Flood Damage, Internal Bickering . . . But the Tourists Still Come in Droves." *Daily News of Los Angeles* 20 June 1999. Valley rop edition: T2.

INDEX

accidents
  airplanes, 91–94
  animal-related, 107–10
  automobiles, 50, 53
  Base jumping, 114–15
  drownings, 83–86, 113
  rockslides, 117–19
Adams, Ansel, x, 69–72
Adams, Virginia Best, 71
Ahwahneechee Miwok Indians, viii, ix,
  5–14, 75
Ahwahnee Hotel, x, 79–82
airplanes, x, 91–94
Anderson, George, 33–36, 95
Anderson, John, 109
The Apron Jam, 117
Arch Rock Fire, 104
Arioli, Peter, 123
Art Photography Company, 46, 47
automobiles, x, 45–49
avalanches, 37–40

Barnes, Tim, 62–63
BASE (Buildings, Antennae, Spans, and
  Earth) jumping, 113–14
bear attacks, 107–10
Berkeley, 77
Berlin Wall, 81
Best, Harry, 71
Best Studio, 71
Big Oak Flats and Yosemite Turnpike
  Company, 21, 22
Big Trees Grove, 23
Black Rock Desert, 91
blizzards, 124–27
Bloody Canyon, 13
Boling, John, 8
Boutkovski, Vladimir, 120–23
Bridalveil Falls, 11

Buchanan, Donald, 63
Bunnell, Lafayette, 7–8, 13
Burnett, Peter, 6–7

Calaveras Big Tree Grove Hotel, 52
California Central Valley, 74
California Magazine, 51
California Sierras, viii, 2–4, 34, 55, 66,
  73, 74
Camp A. E. Wood, 44
Camp Curry, 30, 61, 62, 118, 119
Camp Six, 126–27
Camp Wawona, 44
Castaneda, Carlos, 122
Chickenhead Ledge, 102
Chief Tenaya, 5, 7, 8–9, 10–11, 12,
  13–14, 75
Chinese Camp and Yosemite Turnpike
  Company, 21
Chowchilla Mountain, 20–21
Clark, Galen, 15–18
Colby, William, 65–66
Columbia Tree, 17
Conway, John and sons, 34, 35
Cook, Bruce, 123
Corbett, Mike, 101–2
Cordil, Nicholas, 85
Coulter, George, 21
Coulterville, 20
Coulterville and Yosemite Turnpike
  Company, 21–22
Crane Flat, 21, 22, 66
Cuban Missile Crisis, 81
Curry, David, 29–30

Davis, Jan, 114–15
deer-related accidents, 110

Eagle Rock, 26

earthquakes, 24–27, 119
Edmunds, Emily, 50, 52–53
El Capitan
    accidents, 50, 53
    Ansel Adams, 69, 70–71, 72
    blizzards, 124–27
    climbers, 99–102, 111–12
    naming of, 2, 8
    protestors, 114–15
Ellson, Arthur, 123
erosion, 4
Esteban, Adrian, 96–98
Estes, Jeff, 62
European arrivals, viii
exfoliation of rock, 118–19

Faeghi, Mohammed, 123
Faithful Couple Trees, 17
faulting, 3
Ficery, Michael, 63–64
firsts in Yosemite
    airplane, x
    automobile, x, 45–49
    hotel, x
    humans, viii–ix
    presidential visit, x
Firth, Robert, 96–98
Ford, Henry, 67–68
Foresta, 103–6
forest fires, 103–6
Fort Miller, 12
Fresno River Camp, 6, 8–9
Fuentes, Yolanda and Christine,
    83–85, 86

Gale, G. H. G., 44
Galen Clark Tree, 17
Gambalie, Frank, III, 111–13
Gediman, Scott, 126
General Land Office, 67
geology, vii–viii, 1–4
giant sequoias, ix, 17, 19, 22
Glacier National Parks, 108
Glacier Point, 28, 47–48, 56,
    116–19, 123

Glacier Point Firefall, 28–31, 81
Glacier Point Hotel, 48, 60
Glacier Point Road, 47
Glisky, Jon, 91–94
Goldman, Chris, 85
Gordon, Walter, 62
Grizzly Giant Tree, 17
Grizzly Peak, 83
Guardian of Yosemite, 52

Half Dome
    accidents, 95–98
    and Ansel Adams, 71
    climbers, 95
    first accent, 32–36
    naming of, 2, 8
    suicides, 120–23
    vanishings, 62, 63
hang gliding, 114
Happy Isles Nature Center, 123
Hardage, Karen, 110
Harding, Warren, 100–101, 102
harlequin lupine, 105
Herkomer, Vincent, 123
Herzog, George, 31
Hetch Hetchy, viii, 67, 73–78
Hetch Hetchy Reservoir, 73–78
Hite's Cove, 10, 14
Holliday, Doc, 16
horse-related accidents, 109–10
Hutchings, James Mason, 26, 50–53
Hutchings, John, 109
Hutchings Hotel, 26
hypothermia, 127

Ice Ages and glaciers, viii, 1, 2, 3–4
Inspiration Point, 2, 62
In the Heart of the Sierras (Hutchings), 52

John Muir Wilderness, 99
Johnson, Robert Underwood, 42, 43
Jordan, Brian, 96–98
Juliusson, Kira, 107–9
jumars, 102

Kennedy, John F., x, 79–82
Kerwin, Joseph, 116–18
Kings Canyon, 72
Koenman, Frank, 61–62

Lake Eleanor, 76
Lake May, 62
Lane, Franklin, 67
Lawford, Peter and Patricia, 80
Ledge Trail, 62
Lee Vining, 66
Lewis and Clark Expedition, 43
lightning strikes, 103–6
Lincoln, Abraham, ix, 18, 52
Lippincott, Oliver, x, 46–48, 49
Little Yosemite Valley, 109
Lober, Keith, 124–25
Locomobiles, 45–47
Lodestar Lightning (airplane), 91–94
Lone Pine Earthquake, 24–27
Lower Merced Pass Lake, 92–94
Lujan, Manuel, 106

Mann, William, 16–17
marijuana, 91–94
Mariposa Battalion, ix, 5–9, 19
Mariposa Creek, 6
Mariposa Grove, 17–18, 54, 55
Mariposa (town), 7, 8, 12, 13, 20
Mather, Stephen T., 65–68
McCauley, James, 28–29, 30
McCauley, John and Fred, 29
McGovern, George, 79
McKinley, William, 54
Merced River, viii, 2–3, 83–84, 88–89
miners and settlers, 6, 11–12, 13, 75
Mist Trail, 83
Mono Lake, 12, 66
Moore, Linden, 123
Moore, Treadwell, 12
Mountain House Hotel, 28, 47
Mughir, Richard, 123
Muir, John
    avalanches, 37–40

establishment of Yosemite as a
    national park, 42, 43
and Galen Clark, 15
geology of Yosemite Valley, 3
Hetch Hetchey, 74, 76, 77–78
Lone Pine Earthquake, 24–27
and Theodore Roosevelt, x, 54–58
multi-pitch climbing, 101–2
murders, xi
Murphy Creek Trail, 62

National Park Service, 14, 30–31, 44,
    68, 104–5, 106
Native Americans, viii, ix, 5–14, 75
Nelson, Jeffrey, 91–94
Neu, Colin, 110
Nixon, Richard, 87

Oakland, 77
O'Shaughnessey, Michael, 73–78
O'Shaughnessey Dam, 74, 76, 78
Overhanging Rock, 47–48
Owens Valley Fault, 25

Pacific Coast Borax Company, 66
Panorama Cliffs, 83
Pewing, May, 110
Pillsbury, Arthur, 48
Pioneer Cemetery, 53
pitons and bolts, 100–102
Piute Indians of Mono Lake, 12,
    13–14, 75
Poe, Edgar Allan, 16
Polly Dome Lakes, 62
prospectors. *See* miners and settlers
Pyle, Kerry, 116–18

Raymond, 55
Reinhart, Walter, 63
Rice, Thomas, 96–98
Richmond, 77
Rochette, Chattem, 110
Rock and Bottle Festival, 89
rock climbing, 114

rockslides, 4, 117–19
Roosevelt, Theodore, x, 54–58
Russell, Edward, 46, 47–48, 49
Ryugo, Moriko, 126–27

Sacramento, 6
Sanders, Tom, 114
San Francisco, 20, 25, 67, 75–76, 77
Sargent, Shirley, 105
Savage, James, 5–8
Scenes of Wonder and Curiosity in California (Hutchings), 52
Sentinel Dome, 60
Sequoia National Park, 67, 72
sheep and shepherds, 42, 43–44
Shepherd, F. P., 60–61
siege climbing, 100
Sierra Club, 36, 65, 72, 74
Sierra Nevada. *See* California Sierra
snow blitz, 1, 3
Snow Creek Trail, 62
Spring Valley Water Company, 77
Staircase Falls, 85
Stanley, Francis and Freelan, 45–46
Stanley Steamer, 46
State of California, 21, 41, 57
Stergar, James, 123
Stoneman Meadow Riot, 88–90
suicides, xi, 63, 120–23
Swift Packing Company, 66

Tappan, Clair, 65–66
The Teachings of Don Juan (Castaneda), 122
Tebush, Peter, 116–18, 119
Telescope Tree, 17
Tioga Pass Road, 65–68
Totuya, 13

tourism and tourists, ix–xi, 48–49
traffic, 48–49
Tuolomne River, viii, 14, 76, 77
Turner, Dave, 125–26

Upper Hotel, 52
Upper Yosemite Falls, 85
U.S. Army, 12–13, 41–44, 60–61, 67, 110
U.S. Marines, 63

vanishings, xi, 59–64
Vernal Falls, 83–84
Vietnam War period, 87–90

Walbridge, Garren, 110
Walker, Joseph, viii–ix
Washington Columns, 12
Washington Tree, 17
waterfalls, 3, 83–86
Wawona (town), 43, 47, 55
Wawona Tunnel Overlook, 1–2
Weiner, Bruce, 96–98
Wellman, Marc, 99–102
White Wolf Trail, 63
Whitney, Josiah, x, 3, 26–27, 33, 34
Wondrosek, Godfrey, 62
Wood, Abram Epperson "Jug," 41–42, 43–44

Yamamoto, Ryoichi, 126–27
Yellowstone National Park, 42, 44, 67, 104–5, 108
Yokut Indians, 6
Yosemite Commission, 55–56
Yosemite Falls, 62
Yosemite Valley, vii–viii, 2–4, 42, 57, 75
Yosemite Village, 123

ABOUT THE AUTHORS

Ray Jones is a historian, author, and publishing consultant living in Pebble Beach, California. He has written more than thirty books on subjects ranging from dinosaurs to country stores, but he is probably best known for his lighthouse travel guides and histories. Published by Globe Pequot Press in 2004, his award-winning *Lighthouse Encyclopedia* is widely regarded to be the best and most informative volume on the subject. He has also written a number of PBS companion books including *Windows to the Sea* and *Niagara Falls: An Intimate Portrait,* both also published in 2006 by Globe Pequot Press.

Joe Lubow, formerly Merrill College Librarian and Fellow at the University of California at Santa Cruz, has been an editor and author for more than twenty-five years. His writing has focused mainly on California history, living, and travel. His books with Globe Pequot Press include *Choose a College Town for Retirement* and, more recently, *Disasters and Heroic Rescues of California,* which he cowrote with Ray Jones. Along with writing and editing, Joe spends most of his nights surrounded by books and periodicals as the evening supervisor of the Library at California State University Monterey Bay.